Roman shipping and trade:
Britain and the Rhine provinces

Roman shipping
and trade:
Britain and
the Rhine
provinces

**Edited by
Joan du Plat Taylor
and
Henry Cleere**

1978

Research Report No 24   The Council for British Archaeology

© Authors and The Council for British Archaeology 1978

112 Kennington Road London SE11 6RE

ISBN 0 900312 62 9

Designed by Allan Cooper and Henry Cleere

Printed by Stephen Austin and Sons Ltd,
Hertford, England

Contents

Editors' Foreword

The papers printed in this Report were presented at a Symposium held at the University of Kent, Canterbury, in January 1977. The Symposium was jointly sponsored by the Council for British Archaeology and the Nautical Archaeology Trust. It was the first such joint enterprise between these two bodies, and was designed to bring nautical and 'land-based' archaeologists together for the first time. Programme planning was in the hands of a small working party consisting of Professor Barry Cunliffe, the late Paul Johnstone, Mrs Margaret Rule (Secretary, NAT), and Henry Cleere (Director, CBA); after Paul's untimely death, Mrs Valerie Fenwick joined the working party to represent the NAT.

The Symposium was well attended, and the participants were drawn from a number of western European countries. The discussions on the papers—and, perhaps more important, more informal discussions outside the conference hall—showed how important the initiative taken by the two sponsoring bodies was: it became clear that the two groups were to a large extent unaware of one another's results and problems. It is to be hoped that the contacts established in this way will lead to closer links being formed between nautical and land archaeologists for the joint solution of these and similar problems.

The papers fall into two groups: four papers reporting recent discoveries of boats of the Roman period in the Rhine provinces are followed by a bridging paper on harbours in Britain, which leads into the second group of papers on the archaeological evidence for trade. The final paper, by Dr John Peter Wild, is by way of a summing up of the proceedings, with some valuable observations based on his own work on the textile industry of the Roman period.

Joan du Plat Taylor
Henry Cleere

List of Contributors

Béat Arnold	Départment des Travaux Publics, Musée Cantonal d'Archéologie, 2000 Neuchâtel, Avenue Du Peyrou 7, Switzerland
Henry Cleere	Director, Council for British Archaeology, 112 Kennington Road, London SE11 6RE
Guy De Boe	Service National des Fouilles, Parc du Cinquantenaire 1, B-1040 Brussels, Belgium
M D de Weerd	University of Amsterdam, Albert Egges Van Giffen Instituut voor Prae- en Protohistorie, Singel 453, Amsterdam C, The Netherlands
Detlev Ellmers	Stiftung Deutsches Schiffahrtsmuseum, Van-Ronzelen-Strasse, D-2850 Bremerhaven-M., Federal German Republic
Michael Fulford	Department of Archaeology, University of Reading, Whiteknights, Reading RG6 2AA
Kevin Greene	University of Newcastle upon Tyne, Department of Archaeology, Newcastle upon Tyne NE1 7RU
Mark Hassall	University of London, Institute of Archaeology, 31-34 Gordon Square, London WC1H 0PY
D P S Peacock	Department of Archaeology, The University, Southampton SO9 5NH
Jennifer Price	Salisbury and South Wiltshire Museum, St Ann Street, Salisbury, Wiltshire SP1 2DT
John Peter Wild	University of Manchester, Department of Archaeology, Manchester M13 9PL

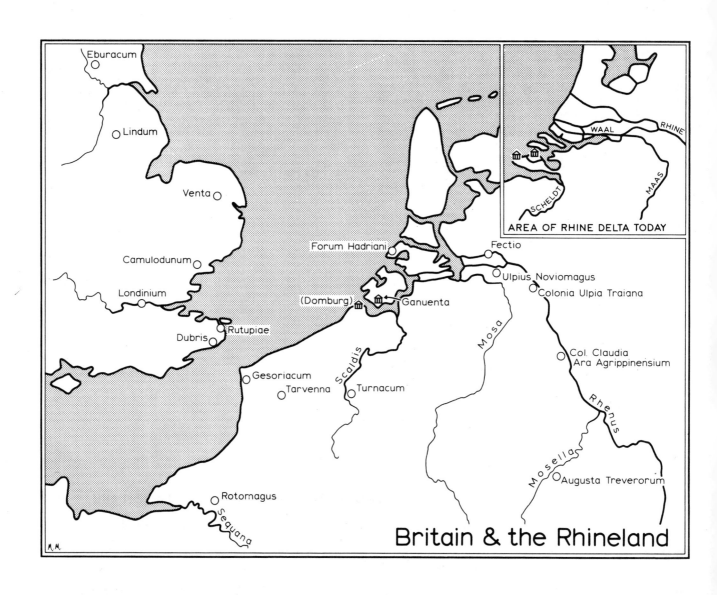

Britain & the Rhineland

M.M.

Eburacum

Lindum

Venta

Camulodunum

Londinium

Dubris

Rutupiae

Gesoriacum

Tarvenna

Turnacum

Scaldis

Forum Hadriani

(Domburg)

Ganuenta

Fectio

Ulpius Noviomagus

Colonia Ulpia Traiana

Col. Claudia
Ara Agrippinensium

Mosa

Rhenus

Mosella

Augusta Treverorum

Rotomagus

Sequana

AREA OF RHINE DELTA TODAY

WAAL

RHINE

SCHELDT

MAAS

viii

Shipping on the Rhine during the Roman period: the pictorial evidence

Detlev Ellmers

The Roman provinces on the Rhine have produced pictorial representations of ships in such numbers that these must be considered as a separate source of evidence in relation to the archaeology of naval architecture (Behn 1911; Moll 1929; Ledroit 1930. None of these surveys was entirely comprehensive at its date. See also Binsfeld 1977). Through this pictorial evidence it is possible to obtain information which neither written sources nor excavated vessels themselves can provide: for example, images of ships on tombstones provide information about shipowners. Evidence is also available about the handling of such ships, their methods of propulsion, the technique of steering, and the numbers of crew. Information about types of ship which have as yet not been discovered in excavations and ideas about the different uses of the various types of vessel can be obtained in this way. The methods of unloading and loading cargo vessels and the handling of warships and fishing boats are also revealed. However, all these pictorial records are only of value for archaeologists and historians when it is possible to identify the types of vessel for which they are valid (Ellmers 1969; 1973; 1976). It was only with the archaeological discoveries made during the 1970s that the basis was laid for this work to be undertaken.

Ship types

The best approach to an understanding of the conditions of shipping during the Roman period is by first considering the indigenous vessels of the pre-Roman Iron Age. As there is no surviving evidence in the regions bordering the Rhine, the conditions found along the upper Danube will have to suffice.

Cargo vessels with open bows (*Bugpforte*)

At the Dürrnberg near Hallein (Ellmers 1969, 84; Reitinger 1975) the grave of a Celtic prince dated to the 5th century BC (early La Tène) contained a miniature gold ship only 65 mm long (Fig 1). This vessel was flat-bottomed, with both stem and stern rising in a flat curve and steep sides; it represents a widely distributed type of river craft which is still common on the Rhine, the Danube, and other continental inland waters at the present time. This type is identified by the following characteristics:

 (i) A trapezoidal plan and a transom bow and stern show that this craft developed from the dugout canoe. The more slender top end of the truck was used as the bow of the vessel, while the wider base end formed the aft section.

 (ii) The transition from the flat bottom of the vessel to the steep sides is rounded, and therefore no sharp angle is present.

 (iii) The open bow (*Bugpforte*) is formed by not curving the flat bottom of the boat at the front up to the same level as the upper edge of the side walls[1]. With this open bow forward the boat was beached like a ferry on the flat river banks. Goods such as barrels could then be loaded by being rolled aboard without having to be lifted over

the ship's sides. In this way rock salt from the Dürrnberg near Hallein was shipped in barrels along the Salzach. It was, however, not possible to construct such an open bow (*Bugpforte*) in a dugout proper, and so to give the vessel sufficient buoyancy it had to be built on a broader keel than a single tree trunk would permit.

A vessel of similar date and cross-section, but with the bow and stern not preserved, was found as early as 1890 on another tributary of the Danube near Ljubljana, then Laibach (Fig 2) (Millner 1892; 1896; Salemke 1973).[2] It demonstrates the standard of boat building, which must be assumed for the 5th century BC cargo vessel from the Dürrnberg. Characteristic for this type of vessel, which is first encountered in a Celtic cultural context and which can still be found to the present day, is the use of the two halves of a dugout, which form the transition from the flat bottom to the relatively steep sides along the whole length of the vessel. These two halves provided the flat-bottomed craft with horizontal stability, which was achieved in Viking ships for example by the construction of a keel. At the same time these half dugouts illustrate the development of this type of boat; a dugout was split lengthwise and heavy bottom planks were fitted in between the two halves. Finally the sides were raised by adding extra strakes. The closing of the stem and stern of a vessel broadened in this way proved difficult; the different methods used in attempts to solve this problem led ultimately to the development of different types of craft.

In the Laibach ship the strakes were joined by a technique of lashing which was in use as early as the Neolithic. In contrast to the relatively weak ribs of the vessels of the earlier periods, the Laibach ship shows two innovations which point to the future: the strong cross-beams used to bind the bottom planks together and the massive angular supports to the sides which were firmly fastened to the side planks by wooden dowels. In place of the later keelson an internal longitudinal plank was fastened with iron nails along the centre of the bottom planks, clenched over and driven back into the wood under the ship's bottom. This type of bond gave the vessel its strength and so made the construction of a relatively large craft possible. Lashing, to which alone the earlier boats owed their stability, was now only used for caulking to make the joints watertight and was later replaced by less labour-intensive caulking techniques (cf the ship finds at Lake Neuenburg, Zwammerdam, and Pommeroeul). The Laibach ship therefore heralds the changeover to carvel-built craft on the continent.

The carvel technique and the dugout halves positioned along the line of transition from the flat bottom of the craft to its sides constitute the basic pattern for continental shipbuilding. Within this general pattern, however, a great variety of ship types can be recognized: eg the cargo vessel shown on a mosaic from Bad Kreuznach, Rheinland-Pfalz (Ellmers 1969, 79-83; 1974, esp 99) which had a sail, an open bow, and a sternpost coiled into a volute (Fig 3).

Fig 1   *Trapeze-shaped cargo boat with two push oars and open bow (Bugpforte) at narrow end. Gold votive boat from grave of a prince from the Dürrnberg near Hallein; 5th century BC. Length 65 mm (Keltenmuseum, Hallein)*

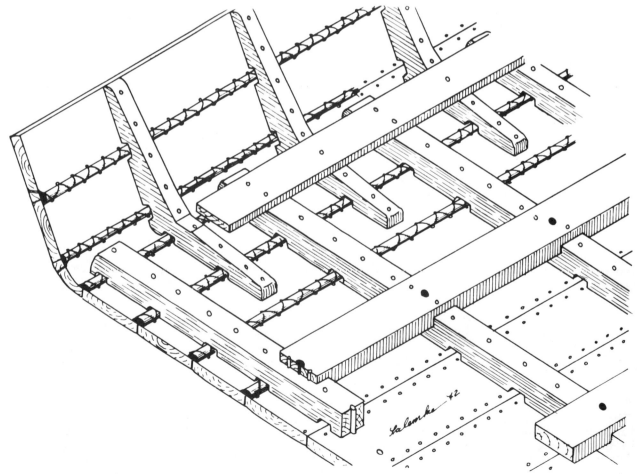

Fig 2   *Schematic reconstruction of ship from Laibach (Ljubljana), Jugoslavia; pre-Roman Iron Age (after G Salemke)*

Fig 3　Cargo vessel with Celtic leather sail, open bow (Bugpforte), and cargo of amphorae; Oceanus mosaic from Bad Kreuznach, Rheinland-Pfalz; c AD 250 (Karl-Geib-Museum, Bad Kreuznach)

The 'Oberländer'

During the late Middle Ages the heavy cargo barges, which originated from the upper Rhine, were known in Cologne as *Oberländer* to distinguish them from the vessels which came from regions lying downstream in the Low Countries. There is no record of the term used for these barges in their area of origin or for their name during the Roman period. However, it is now possible to reconstruct the history of their development: the two cargo dugouts, each about 11 m long, found at Austruweel near Antwerp (Ellmers 1972, 110-11 & 287-8 (Cat no 35 i-j))[3] belong to the pre-Roman Iron Age or to the early Roman period and mark the beginning of this development (Fig 4). The determining characteristics of this type of craft are the retained rounded cross-section combined with a trapeze-shaped plan, with the top of the

trunk serving as the bow. By contrast with the majority of the central European dugouts, where a certain amount of the original wood was retained to close off each end of the hollowed-out trunk, here the trunk was dug out completely and then closed by inserting vertically set semi-circular boards which were nailed to either end. This gave the heavy dugouts, which were reinforced by transverse frames, a rather clumsy and almost box-like appearance.

From this type of dugout the *Oberländer* was then constructed by splitting the trunk lengthwise and inserting bottom planks[4] between the two halves; the boards nailed to the stern and bow only needed to be widened to accommodate the new dimensions. By nailing the board at the bow, the so-called *Kaffe*, in a sloping plane, it was possible to land the boat on a shallow river bank. A tombstone at Mainz, dating to the middle of the 1st century AD, shows the boatman Blussus (Fig 5) at the helm of such a vessel (Ellmers 1973, 29-30; 1976, 12-15 & 39-42). The height of the stern, which is formed by the base of the trunk, has been exaggerated.

The punt (Nachen) and related types

To understand the elongated oval plan of the punt (*Nachen*) it is necessary to consider the construction of punt-like dugouts: the upward-facing part of the tree trunk was worked into a horizontal plane, which rose towards either end to allow the boat to ride the waves more easily (Fig 6). For the construction of a symmetrical dugout this horizontal plane was vital, because it provided the starting point for hollowing out the interior of the trunk. At the same time the intersection of this plane with the outer surface of the trunk defined the plan of the craft, the base of the trunk being used as the bow end. The sides of the boat were worked, according to type, either vertically or at an inclined angle. In each case, however, the punt had a flat bottom with an inclined plane at either end of the boat (Fig 7). If it was necessary to increase the height of the sloping sides of a craft, an additional strake was nailed to the upper edge of the boat in such a way that it formed an angle with the side wall below. In this way it was possible to nail through the full thickness of the plank and down into the wood of the trunk. The cross-section of such a boat forms five sides of an octagon (cf Fig 8b). By splitting the dugout lengthwise and inserting bottom planks the boat could be widened, and finally a further strake could be added, again at an angle to the previous one. This stage

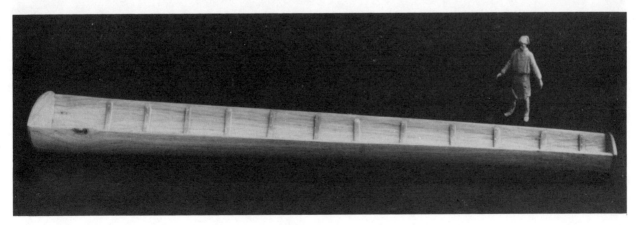

Fig 4　Model of cargo dugout from Antwerp-Austruweel; pre-Roman or Roman Iron Age. Original 11 m in length (Deutsches Schiffahrtsmuseum, Bremerhaven)

Fig 5   *Drifting cargo vessel of Oberländer type, with steering oars at bow and stern, two pairs of oars, and a short mast for towing. Relief from tombstone of the boatman Blussus from Mainz; mid 1st century AD (Mittelrheinisches Landesmuseum, Mainz)*

Fig 6   *Model to demonstrate development of punt-type boat (Nachen) from tree-trunk (Deutsches Schiffahrts-museum, Bremerhaven)*

of construction is shown on a boat-shaped pottery lamp (with the figurine of a dog) which was found at Weissenburg in Bavaria (Fig 8a).[5] The kinks in the outer shell are clearly visible.

For some types of craft built to this design, it was already known how to construct the side wall without the kink, as is testified by some boat finds which use a pure carvel technique with several strakes fitted on top of one another. The pictorial representations are not always clear enough to decide with certainty whether a type with or without kink is being shown, but the marked incline in the plane of the gunwale makes it possible to differentiate between a punt-like vessel (Fig 9) (*Trierer Zeitschrift*, **11** (1936), 225 & fig 19; Binsfeld 1977, 3, pl 1.2) and the *Oberländer*, which has a horizontal gunwale (Fig 5).

Cargo barges with inward-pointing bow and stern

Clearly distinct from the boats discussed so far, with their relatively low shapes, are those types in which the ends of stem and stern are vertical or even bent backwards towards the boat itself (Fig 10). It is not so easy to identify this rounded type among the known ship finds as it is with the previous types. The fragmentary vessel from Yverdon, Switzerland, may be reconstructed in this rounded fashion. The remaining lower section shows clearly the beginning of a pronounced rounded, upturning curve with the bottom planks overlapping at this point (*Helvetia Archaeologica*, **19/20** (1974), 70-8, 102). There are indications, however, that it will soon be possible to describe the construction of this type of vessel more accurately with the help of newly discovered ship remains, since it has only been during the present decade that other important finds have been made.

Seagoing cargo vessels of native construction

So far no pictorial representations are known of seagoing craft of native construction, comparable with the ship found at Blackfriars, London.

Seagoing cargo vessels of Mediterranean construction

Seagoing cargo vessels of Mediterranean construction are pictured on several 4th century gilt glass bowls from a workshop, possibly in Cologne.[6] These bowls depict, among several scenes from the Old Testament, the story of the prophet Jonah being thrown from a merchant ship into the sea and then swallowed by a sea monster (Fig 11). By contrast with most other cases of representations of ships, these pictures are not describing an everyday event, but tell a literary story using a pictorial concept that is strongly influenced by Mediterranean traditions. In spite of their origin at a workshop in Cologne, these representations might easily be dismissed as repetitions of a Mediterranean design. But in fact each of the three known Jonah scenes from Cologne shows a different type of ship, and so it may be assumed that the artisans based themselves when depicting a ship on a type known to them in Cologne. That ships of Mediterranean construction may have visited the Rhine has already been proved by the earliest ship find, which has been reasonably well documented. This ship displayed the characteristic mortise-and-tenon construction, but this technique was not recognized as Mediterranean in the late 19th century. This boat was only small, but the ship at County Hall in London, which was constructed in the same way, proves that large merchant vessels of Mediterranean construction were used in the trade with Britannia (Ellmers 1972, 293 (Cat no 45) & 277 (Cat no 15d)).

The ships on the gold glass bowls, however, are unfortunately drawn with so little detail that it is very difficult to allocate them to a specific type.

The bowl from St Ursula in Cologne shows a large sea-going vessel with a square-rigged mainsail of Mediterranean type (Lat *velum*), plus an additional small rectangular sail on the forecastle. The ship on the glass from Cologne-Braunsfeld (Fig 11) has a rounded hull with its main sail (*velum*) secured by clew-lines. A steering oar is visible at the side, and amidships some

Fig 7   Model of punt-shaped dugout with ribs from Hamburg; Middle Ages. Original 5.94 m long (Deutsches Schiffahrtsmuseum, Bremerhaven)

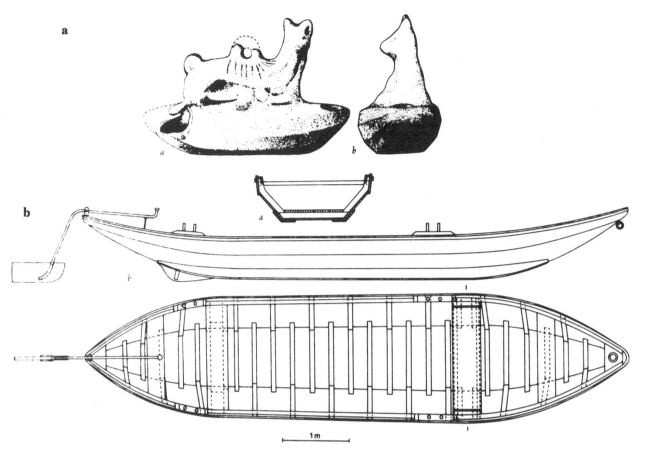

Fig 8   a Punt-shaped clay lamp from Weissenburg, Bavaria; 2nd century AD (Weissenburg Museum). b 20th century punt, middle Rhine region, 8 m long (Wasserstrassenmaschinenamt, Koblenz)

Fig 9   Punt-shaped boat with steering oars at stern and bow and cargo of wine. The central boatman has tapped one of the barrels and is drinking wine through a straw. Cast with a fragmentary pottery mould from Trier; 4th century AD. Width 139 mm (Rheinisches Landesmuseum, Trier)

Fig 10   Barge with cargo of bales of cloth, which is being towed. Relief from tombstone at Igel, near Trier; c AD 250

oars may be detected. The question as to whether sea-going merchant ships were equipped for rowing still needs further investigation. Finally, the gold glass bowl from St Severin in Cologne shows a rowing boat without sails.

Warships of Mediterranean construction

There are numerous pictorial representations of ships belonging to the Roman fleet on the Rhine. But in the case of the best known pictorial evidence, the famous wine ships from Neumagen (Fölzer 1911; Loeschke 1927: cf Behn 1911; Moll 1929; Ledroit 1930), the ship type has invariably been wrongly identified. The cargo of wine barrels has masked the fact that these were warships which had been detailed for wine transport. Great confusion has been caused by the fact that the figures are shown too large in proportion to the size of the ship (Fig 12). Through this distortion scholars have for a long time overlooked the fact that the crew of this wine transport has to be depicted as standing on the fighting deck of the ship, the upper edge of which was located immediately beneath the lattice work of the bulwark. Below the fighting deck the enclosed banks of oars accommodated the large number of rowers needed to work the 22 oars on each side. This meant at least 44 men if each oar was worked by one person (and double this number if each oar needed two rowers). When the fourteen-man crew plus two helmsmen are added, it becomes apparent that it took at least 60 men to transport at the most fourteen barrels of wine (cf p 13). This would have bankrupted a private merchant since his competitors were able to transport at least eight barrels of wine with a crew of only three. On this tombstone, therefore, the merchant was not portraying his own ship, but was indicating to posterity that he was the supplier of wine to the army or the navy.

Finally, research into shipping has missed the fact that, apart from the large ships, there are also smaller vessels pictured in the evidence from Neumagen. These ships are not as well preserved, but they too display in their upper cargo layer a row of four wine barrels. The accompanying crew may have been cut by two. This type of vessel, although portrayed in an identical manner, may therefore have been slightly shorter, but on no account was it only half the size of the big wine ship, which had underneath its fighting deck accommodation for double the number of oars compared with the smaller ship, 22 and 11 respectively.

This observation provides the determining criterion for the typological identification of both vessels: the smaller wine ship is a *monere* with only one bank of oars beneath the fighting deck, whilst the large wine ship is a *bireme* with two banks of oars beneath the fighting deck. Constantius Chlorus sailed with a fleet comprised of oar-driven warships of the Neumagen type from the Rhine to Britannia where, after victories over Carausius and Allectus, he had himself acclaimed in London as the 'Restorer of the Eternal Light'. A gold medallion was struck at Trier to commemorate these events.[7]

There are several other portrayals of warships from the area along the Rhine, but these lack the raised animal head at the bow. The number of oars shown is also too

Fig 11   Seagoing merchantman of Mediterranean construction with linen sail and oars. Central medallion on gold glass bowl from Köln-Braunsfeld; first half of 4th century AD. 51 mm diameter (Römisch-Germanisches Museum, Köln)

Fig 12   Bireme with ram, 22 oars, and one steering oar on each side (damaged), plus cargo of wine barrels on fighting deck. Tombstone from Neumagen/Mosel; first quarter of 3rd century AD (Rheinisches Landes-museum, Trier)

Fig 13   *Anglo-Saxon warship with helmsman at bow and stern and seven pairs of oarsmen. Pottery fragment from Trier; first half of 4th century AD. 167 mm long (Rheinisches Landesmuseum, Trier)*

small, and so it is not possible to decide between a *monere, bireme,* or even *trireme* (with three banks of oars). These vessels are, however, equipped with a large square sail (La Baume 1968, 108, pl 9; Behn 1911; Moll 1929; Ledroit 1930).

Finally, there are representations of warships which carry above the ram an additional beam, richly decorated, which was intended to protect the ship from damage by a rammed opponent (Exhibition guide Middelburg 1971, Deae Nehalenniae, altar no 13 (*c* AD 200)). Four finds of decorated bronze beam mounts have been made in the Rhine so far (Ellmers 1972, Cat no 57, 60a & 62a; plus one example in a private collection). Wooden remains of those warships have not yet been discovered, but in theory the mortise-and-tenon method of construction would be expected in these cases.

Warships of Germanic construction

Colleagues in Britain may be greatly interested to learn that Germanic warships are portrayed on the vertical outer surfaces of two samian bowls of the Gose 62 type from Trier which date to the first half of the 4th century (Binsfeld 1977, 1-3 & pl 2; Ellmers 1975, 79-90, esp 84), as two fragments of differing styles show (Fig 13). Characteristic of the Germanic warships is the manning by a large number of rowers along the sides of the ship, a feature which is well known from Scandinavian rock drawings as early as the Bronze Age. The point of interest about the evidence from Trier sherds is the fact that in the early 4th century the use of loose paddles continued unchanged. The streamlined boats themselves are known through finds from Scandinavia and North Germany. They were artificially widened dugouts of

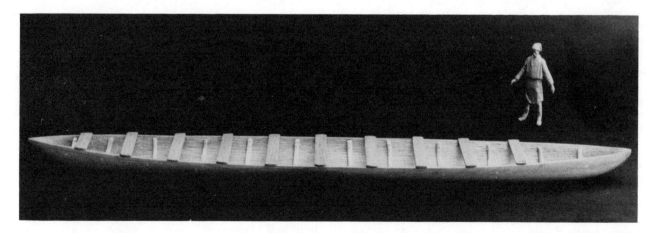

Fig 14   *Model of Germanic warship with seating for helmsman at bow and stern and eight pairs of oarsmen. Artificially widened dugout from Vaaler Moor, Schleswig-Holstein; c 1st-3rd century AD. Original 12.29 m long (Deutsches Schiffahrtsmuseum, Bremerhaven)*

Fig 15   Cargo vessel propelled by punting, with nearly vertical steering oar at stern and cargo of wine barrels. Fragment of altar from temple of Nehalennia, goddess of seafarers, from Colijnsplaat, Netherlands; c AD 200. 0.46 m wide (Leiden Museum)

lanceolate plan with their sides heightened by one or two additional strakes using the clinker technique. These carried a large number of seats for the rowers (Fig 14). Accordingly no evidence for the existence of tholes for oars can be detected. These appear for the first time at the end of the 4th century in the Nydam boat and indicate a great technological advance in ship propulsion which probably only became common during the second half of the 4th century.

As to why typical Germanic warships were portrayed at Trier, it must be remembered that Trier was the central headquarters from which the campaign against the Anglo-Saxon pirates was organized. The pottery reliefs from Trier are thus the earliest known representatives of Anglo-Saxon warships.

Propulsion and steering gear
The mode of propulsion used in warships has already been discussed, as it is one of the determining characteristics for this type of ship. With the merchantmen on the Rhine and its tributaries it was not so usual to restrict a specific method of propulsion to any one type of vessel; it was not uncommon to find several methods used on the same craft, eg towing only when going upstream and simple drifting when going downstream.

Punting (Ellmers 1972, 83-7)
It was possible, especially in shallow waters, to propel boats by pushing long poles into the firm ground below the surface of the water and move in this way either upstream or downstream. The speed when going upstream depended on the strength of the current, but it was possible in this way to proceed without special installations along the bank, such as towpaths. As all that was needed to make this method effective was a long wooden pole, it may be assumed to be of great antiquity, even though there is no certain pre-Roman evidence. From the Roman period at least, the business end of the pole was sheathed with iron to reduce wear. Using the different types of sheathing (spout-, prong-, disc-, or hook-shaped as well as combination with an oar-blade), it would be possible to sort the numerous finds of mounts

into type groups, but this aspect will not be discussed at the present time when the method of their use is the prime concern.

The punter could be permanently stationed at one point on the boat (usually at the stern): he would push the pole into the river or lake bed and then push himself and the boat forward by gripping along the pole. The version of the punting pole which ended in an oar-blade was used in the same way but in deep stretches of water it could double as a large paddle. There are also pictures which show it in use as an additional steering oar at the bow.

More commonly portrayed is the method of punting in which the pole is furnished with a crutch-like handle (Ellmers 1976, 72-88). The punter would push his pole alongside the boat into the bottom of the river, then tuck the crutch under his arm and push the boat along by walking with his back towards the direction of travel from bow to stern (Fig 15). A prerequisite for this method was the introduction of an inside walking plank along the entire length of the ship wall (cf the ship found at Pommeroeul). When punting in this way a helmsman was needed to keep the boat on course.

Towing (Ellmers 1972, 82-3; *Trierer Zeitschrift,* 11 (1936), 225-7, & fig 18)
Although the construction and maintenance of towpaths along river banks required an extensive organization, ships have been towed up-river on the Rhine and the Moselle since the Roman period. It was, however, human traction that was employed (Fig 10); there is no evidence for the use of horses. The tow-line was fastened either at the bow (Fig 10) or at a special short mast on the forecastle (Fig 5). A helmsman on board had to steer the ship clear of the banks.

Paddling or rowing (Ellmers 1975)
The development of the indigenous method of rowing has been well researched.

During the 5th century BC it was already common practice in the area north of the Alps to propel comparatively small boats with one or two push oars which were fastened by loops made of rope or willow to the sides of the vessel (Fig 1). The oarsman faced forward and pushed the oar handle away from himself, which in turn pushed the blade of the oar backwards through the water and thus propelled the boat forwards. To return the oar to its starting position it was necessary to turn the oar through 90° and pull its narrow edge forward through the water. With a slight turn of the blade during the working stroke it was possible to steer the boat at the same time. On Alpine lakes and with the Venetian gondola this technique is still in use today.

The introduction of the pull oar (*Riemen*) is, as the term indicates (Lat *remus*), of Roman origin and occurred in the Rhineland very soon after the Roman occupation began (Fig 5). With this innovation the two tasks carried out by the man working the old push oar were now distributed to different people: steering was now done by the helmsman, while the propulsion was produced by the rowers, who were now seated with their backs towards the bow, working the oars set in tholes on the gunwale.

The oars and paddles of Roman and Germanic warships have been discussed on pp 7-10.

Drifting (Ellmers 1972, 82; 1975)

If the vessel was allowed to drift with the river current, no other method of propulsion was really necessary. During the Roman period, however, additional means of propulsion (eg the oar: Fig 5) were employed to increase speed. Definitive evidence for the use of drifting is provided by the fact that the ship is practically stationary in the surrounding water: ie no water is flowing past the steering oar. An additional steering oar is therefore required at the bow to help steer the ship away from shallows, rocks, and other obstacles (Fig 5). This steering oar at the bow is a sure indication of the use of drifting. From the 5th century BC (Fig 1) onwards until modern times this method has been used in its differing forms on the Rhine.

Sailing (Ellmers 1969; 1974; 1975)

When discussing the Roman warship it has already been mentioned that some of these ships carried a sail in the form of the Mediterranean *velum*. This was a rectangular linen sail, suspended from a yard arm which was hoisted at the mast.

Two representations of the Celtic leather sail, as it was described by Caesar, have been identified in the Rhineland, where on a mosaic at Bad Kreuznach alongside the grey cloth sail of the warship the other type has been reproduced in a yellow-brown colour. The leather sail uses, beside the yard arm, several additional transverse beams plus a lower boom (Fig 3). It was used on river craft (cargo vessel with open bow) as well as on seagoing ships.

Methods of steering (Ellmers 1975; 1976, 82-8)

When discussing drifting as a means of propulsion the steering oar at the bow (which was indispensable in this case) has already been mentioned.

The development of the native steering technique started with a push oar attached at the stern of the boat (see pp 10-11), enabling the ship to be propelled and steered at the same time. When these two functions were separated and allotted to different people the helmsman put his oar over the stern obliquely into the water and was thus able to steer. A simple notch in the stern prevented the loom of the oar from slipping and, by inventing a vertically

suspended tiller (Fig 5), it became possible to increase the size of the loom and thereby the leverage. A steering oar of this type was found in Lake Neuenburg near Bevaix in 1911 (*Helvetia Archaeologica,* **19/20** (1974), 90). The next step in the development is documented on an altar dedicated to the goddess Nehalennia dating to around AD 200 from Colijnsplaat in Holland (Fig 15) (Exhibition guide Middelburg 1971, altar no 44).

By suspending the loom more securely it was possible to give the steering oar a nearly vertical position and the tiller a horizontal one. From this type of steering oar it was only a small step to the stern rudder used in the medieval Hanseatic *cog*; all that was needed was to position an additional fixing point between the sternpost and the rudder in the shape of a rudder pintle and rudder eye. At what point in time this step was taken is as yet not known.

Warships and merchantmen built on the Rhine to Mediterranean specifications display the well known Mediterranean steering oars fixed to both sides of the ship (Fig 12). Two helmsmen were therefore needed to steer these ships. One such steering oar has been found near Zwammerdam (De Weerd 1978); it had been constructed, like other Mediterranean planking, with mortise-and-tenon joints. It is possible that this type of side steering oar had also been adopted by native cargo vessels. The tombstone from Igel near Trier shows a similar side oar with tiller (Fig 10).

The Germanic side steering oar was at this time still quite different in construction. It was a simple paddle (Fig 13), which only later developed into the somewhat comparable side steering oar with tiller as used on the Viking ships (Ellmers 1975, 83ff).

The crew (Ellmers 1972, 263-5)

Whilst the crew of a Roman warship used as transport vessel may be assumed to be at least 60 men strong (*bireme*) (Fig 12) or 36 (*monere*), and the Germanic warship carried at least a crew of 16, the manpower used on a cargo vessel in the inland trade was considerably smaller. Owing to the lack of pictorial evidence it is not possible to make similar assumptions for the seagoing merchantman.

In principle it was possible on inland waters for one man, with the help of a punting pole or push oar, to handle a small cargo vessel by himself, when going upstream as well as downstream. Larger vessels carried from the 5th century BC onwards an additional man during the downstream journey, who handled the steering oar at the bow (Fig 1) and naturally helped with punting during the journey upstream. But the usual crew of a cargo vessel on the Rhine during the Roman period was three men: one helmsman and one man on either side of the craft using the type of punting pole which tucked under the arm (Fig 15); a helmsman and two men for towing, when towing was used (Fig 10); one helmsman (omitted in the picture, but necessary) as well as two men to work the sails, if it was a cargo vessel driven by sail (Fig 3); and finally one man each at the stern oar and the bow oar plus one man as relief in a cargo boat drifting downstream (Fig 9). In the example just mentioned the relief may have used his spare time for a drink from one of the wine barrels, using a straw for this purpose! In customs regulations dating from about AD 900 a three-man crew was still assumed to be the norm for cargo vessels[8].

Naturally larger crews are known for inland vessels on the Rhine, but it is impossible to comment on how often larger crews were used, since among the relatively few

a

b

Fig 16   Dockers rolling barrels aboard and carrying sacks ashore. Two fragments from tombstone at Mainz, c AD 200
(Mittelrheinisches Landesmuseum, Mainz)

pictorial representations most show three-man crews, with only one six-man crew. The *Oberländer* belonging to Blussus was represented as being an especially large vessel by showing one man each at the stern and bow oars as well as two pairs of oarsmen (Fig 5). In fact, during the Middle Ages the *Oberländer* was the largest cargo vessel on the middle stretches of the Rhine; at that time, however, it carried a crew of up to seventeen (two helmsmen at the stern, five at the bow, and ten men at the oars).

Transfer of goods

Whilst the draught of the vessels can best be calculated from the ship finds and information about the goods transported can be obtained from written sources, the pictorial representations are the best evidence for cargo handling and harbour use. The most common form of packing was the barrel (Figs 9, 12, 15, 16). The contents may be assumed to be wine, especially if one of the barrels is shown being tapped. Salt, because of its solubility in water, was also transported in barrels, apparently as early as the 5th century BC when special ships with open bows were used which allowed the barrels simply to be rolled aboard (Fig 1). The harbour installation needed for this type of ship was merely a sloping river bank on to which the open bow of the boat could be beached (Pirling & Ellmers 1972; Ellmers 1976, 48-50; Ulbert 1959). With other types of ship the barrels had to be laboriously rolled aboard along a gangway and over the ships' sides. This required two men for each barrel (Fig 16a). On the open boats the barrels were stacked either lengthwise or crosswise, apparently in two layers. Figure 9 indicates a lower line of barrels lying in pairs lengthwise inside the ship. To ensure that the top pair, which were stacked crosswise, would lie securely three lower pairs of barrels were needed. The entire load may therefore be considered to be eight barrels. Correspondingly, underneath the four visible barrels on the wineships from Neumagen a layer of five pairs must be assumed, which would mean a load of fourteen barrels in all (Fig 12). On the altar from Colijnsplaat (Fig 15) both layers of barrels lie apparently across the ship, and so the ship apparently carried eight barrels.

The second most common means of packaging appearing in pictorial representations is the amphora (Fig 13), the typically Mediterranean form of container without a standing base. North of the Alps it was mainly shipped during the Roman period. Before and after this period, however, barrels formed a large part of ships' cargoes. During transport the amphorae were wrapped in plaited straw, similar to present-day carboys. To keep them upright frameworks were erected on shore into which one layer of amphorae was set. A further layer could be fitted into the gaps between the necks of this layer until whole pyramids of amphorae were standing on the quays waiting for further transport (eg Loeschke 1933, pl I.1 & V.1 & 2). Aboard the ships, too, the amphorae had to be kept upright. Whether similar frameworks existed aboard ship cannot as yet be established. Perhaps the ships' sides and a few loose transverse boards provided the necessary stability for these vessels. In any case they were stacked on top of each other on board too, as a relief fragment from Trier shows. There is no pictorial evidence from the Rhineland of how they were taken aboard; there are, however, pictures from the Mediterranean, which show one man carrying a single amphora on his shoulders, holding on to its handles while negotiating a narrow gangway on to the ship.[9]

The tombstone of a cloth merchant from Igel near Trier shows the transport of tied bales of cloth, which had been piled in the open ships in two layers, like the barrels, in such a way that above the tightly packed bottom layer two bales can be seen above the ship's side (Fig 10). Unfortunately there is no pictorial evidence of how these bales were taken aboard. It is impossible that one man would have been able to carry one of these bales on his shoulders. It can only be assumed that a kind of planking slipway was used by means of which the bales were dragged over the ship's side.

Finally, a tombstone fragment from Mainz (Behn 1911, 420; Ledroit 1930, 20) shows a line of men carrying full sacks on their shoulders across a gangway on to the shore (Fig 16b). To judge from the shape of the sacks they seem to contain grain or something similar. The large number of men, who are seen to leave the ship one after the other and return via a second gangway (not visible in the fragment) after depositing their sacks, would imply a gang of dockers. The number of the crew proper would certainly have been much smaller.

It is certainly no accident that it is the loading and unloading of barrels and sacks which is depicted on the tombstone from Mainz. The same combination of barrel and sack recurs in an inscription on a tombstone from Trier, ordered by a *cuparius et saccarius* named Julius Victor (Loeschke 1933, 24-5). As barrels and sacks are manufactured by two completely different processes, it can only be assumed that the professions named on the tombstone refer to the process of loading. As it is most unlikely that a mere porter of sacks and barrels would have been able to afford an expensive tombstone, the *cuparius et saccarius* will therefore more likely have been the proprietor or supervisor of a shipping firm in the port of Trier. A similar function may be assumed for his colleague from Mainz, who had scenes of his business activities carved on his tombstone. How far such a business would have had depots elsewhere has still to be examined.

Unfortunately there are no pictures from the Roman period showing the transport of stone on water, although there is archaeological evidence for transportation of large quantities of stones in Roman times (Röder 1970). Large blocks of stone were apparently the heaviest goods transported by ship at this time. Next came large barrels of 1.5-2 m in length and 0.74-1 m in diameter. While barrels were rolled and blocks of stone as well as bales were dragged on board ship, lighter pieces (amphorae, sacks) were carried on board on the shoulders of large numbers of porters. There is no evidence from the Roman period for the use of cranes, which became characteristic for the ports along the Rhine during the Middle Ages.

A surprising factor is that on all open river craft which have been portrayed the cargo is uniform in its composition (on seagoing vessels with a deck the cargo is not visible). Mixed loads of ingots and barrels, or barrels and amphorae, cannot be detected anywhere. During the early medieval period the uniformity of the cargo on river craft has been documented on several occasions (Ellmers 1972, 260). It can therefore be assumed to have been the norm. The specialization of merchants in particular goods such as fish sauces (*negotiatores allecari*), ceramics (*neg cretarii*), salt (*neg salarii*), wine (*neg vinarii*), etc which is noticeable in Roman inscriptions may indicate that river craft normally transported only the goods of one merchant at a time. Whether seagoing vessels carried a mixed cargo cannot be ascertained. At any rate the merchants using seagoing craft were not identified according to a specific kind of merchandise, but commonly by the country with whom they were trading, eg *negotiatores Britanniciani*. On the other hand, there is no rule without an exception and there exists among the inscriptions from Colijnsplaat one by a trader with Britannia who stated his specialization in ceramics (Exhibition guide Middelburg 1971, altar no 11).

A final observation may follow from this. On the votive tablets at Colijnsplaat which were dedicated to the goddess of seafarers, Nehalennia, several river craft and their long oars are portrayed. There is only one representation of the steering oar of a seagoing ship. From this one may conclude that it was just possible for river craft to reach this furthest point at the mouth of the river. Here was the end of their journey and at this point the goods destined for Britannia had to be transferred on to seagoing vessels. One can be sure that the siting of the temple was a result of the transfer of the trading post to this spot from another point on the river. Domburg on Walcheren, because of a change in the course of the river. But if many river craft went as far as Colijnsplaat, not many seagoing vessels sailed beyond this point further upriver.

A further question which has to be considered concerns the extent to which the merchants owned the ships as opposed to only providing the cargo. The pictorial tombstones point to the latter assumption. The portrayal of the wine ship from Neumagen (Fig 12) shows most clearly that the vessel did not belong to the wine merchant who was embellishing his tombstone with it; and the merchant who, at Junkerath, high up in the Eifel mountains and miles away from any navigable water, had a large sailing ship chiselled on to his tombstone (Ellmers 1969, 51-3) did not want to claim the ownership of the vessel but wanted to indicate his far-flung trading connections.

(Translated by Katrin Aberg)

References

Behn, F, 1911   Römische Schiffe in Deutschland, *Alterthümer unserer heidnischen Vorzeit,* **5,** 417ff.

Binsfeld, W, 1977   Moselschiffe, *Festschrift für W Haberey,* 1-3.

Dammann, W, 1974   Rheinschiffe aus Krefeld und Zwammerdam, *Das Logbuch,* **10,** 1, 4-10.

Dove, C E, 1971   The first British navy, *Antiquity,* **45,** 15-20.

Ellmers, D, 1969   Keltischer Schiffbau, *Jahrbuch des Römisch-Germanischen Zentralmuseums Mainz,* **16,** 73-122.

——, 1972   *Frühmittelalterliche Handelsschiffahrt in Mittel- und Nordeuropa.*

——, 1973   Rheinschiffe der Römerzeit, *Beiträge zur Rheinkunde,* **2,** Folge 25, 25-41.

——, 1974   Vor- und frühgeschichtliche Schiffahrt am Nordrand der Alpen, *Helvetia Archaeologica,* **19/20,** 94-104.

——, 1975   Antriebstechniken germanischer Schiffe im 1. Jahrtausend n Chr, *Deutsches Schiffahrtsarchiv,* **1,** 75-90.

——, 1976   *Kogge, Kahn und Kunststoffboot, Führer des Deutschen Schiffahrtsmuseums,* 7.

Fölzer, E, 1911   Ein Neumagener Schiff neu ergänzt, *Bonner Jahrbucher,* **120,** 236-50.

La Baume, P, 1968   Römische Bernsteinarbeiten in Köln, in *Studien zur europäischen Vor- und Frühgeschichte.*

Ledroit, J, 1930   *Die römische Schiffahrt im Stromgebiet des Rheins, Kulturgeschichtlicher Wegweiser durch das Römisch-Germanische Zentralmuseum,* 12.

Loeschke, S, 1927   Der zweite Tierkopf zum Neumagener Moselschiff, *Trierer Zeitschrift,* **2,** 105-12.

——, 1933   *Denkmäler vom Weinbau aus der Zeit der Römerherrschaft an Mosel, Saar und Ruwer.*

Millner, A, 1892   Ein Schiff im Laibacher Moore, *Argo, Zeitschrift für krainische Landeskunde,* **1,** 1-7.

——, 1896   Addendum, *ibid,* **5.**

Moll, F, 1929   *Das Schiff in der bildenden Kunst.*

Pirling, R, & Ellmers, D, 1972   Ein mittelalterliches Schiff aus dem Rhein, *Die Heimat,* **43,** 45-8.

Reitinger, J, 1975   Das goldene Miniaturschiffchen vom Dürrnberg bei Hallein, *Mitteilungen der Gesellschaft Salzburger Landeskunde,* **115,** 383-405.

Röder, J, 1970   Die mineralischen Baustoffe der römischen Zeit im Rheinland, *Bonner Universitätsblätter,* 1970, 6-19.

Salemke, G, 1973   Die Ausgrabung eines Binnensee-Transportschiffes, *Das Logbuch,* **9,** 1, 21-4.

Ulbert, G, 1959   Römische Holzfässer aus Regensburg, *Bayerische Vorgeschichtsblätter,* **24,** 6-29.

Weerd, M D De, 1978   Römerzeitliche Transportschiffe und Einbäume aus Nigrum Pullum/Zwammerdam, Niederlande, *Akten des 10. internationalen Kongresses für Limesforschungen,* 187-98.

Notes

[1] The open bow (*Bugpforte*) was first identified on the ship find from Krefeld, 1972 (Pirling & Ellmers 1972).

[2] With regard to the technological position of this ship see Ellmers 1976, 15-17.

[3] With regard to the tradition of ship building see Ellmers 1976, 45-8.

[4] This construction was first identified in a medieval *Oberländer* from Krefeld, 1973 (Dammann 1974).

[5] First published in *Obergermanisch-Rätischer Limes,* **72** (1906), 55, pl 11.55. See also Ellmers 1969, 89-91.

[6] Clearly arranged in the guide of the Römisch-Germanische Museum, Köln: *Frühchristliches Köln,* 1965, 67-73, pls 10 & 12.

[7] Starting with this new point of reference the interpretation of the coin pictures in Dove 1971 should be closely reexamined.

[8] Zollbestimmung von Raffelstetten an der oberen Donau: *Monumenta Germaniae historica,* Capitularia II, No 253, § 7.

[9] Mosaic from Ostia, published in *Helvetia Archaeologica,* **19/20** (1974), dust jacket.

Ships of the Roman period at Zwammerdam / Nigrum Pullum, Germania Inferior

M D de Weerd

In 1968-71 the Instituut voor Prae- en Protohistorie of the University of Amsterdam excavated a Roman auxiliary fort (Fig 17) on the south bank of the river Rhine, *limes* of the Empire between AD 47 and 260. There were three periods: (a) AD 47-69, timber buildings of military character; (b) AD 70-*c* 175, a wooden fort; (c) AD 175-260, a stone fort, foundations of a bath building, and part of a *vicus* and long rows of Flavian quays, extended twice in the 2nd century. The report on the excavations was published by Haalebos (1973; 1977).

In December 1971 a dugout was found by accident and heavily damaged, but a new series of excavations was undertaken which ended in July 1974. In addition to the usual archaeological finds, attention was focused on what proved to be of importance to the history of ship construction: three dugouts, three large barges, and one steering oar, all embedded in river deposits and dated by small finds to about AD 150-225. Work on dating problems is still in progress. Except for the first dugout, all the ships and the steering oar are to be preserved in the Museum of Nautical Archaeology in Ketelhaven by the State Service for Polder Reclamation, Lelystad. Research on wood conservation is undertaken by this State Service (De Jong 1977). All the ships were built of oak, but some elements of the dugouts are of silver fir, *Abies alba*.

Zwammerdam has now shown that the oldest type of barge, up to 1972 known only from the 6th-8th century AD (Ellmers 1972, 95: barge at Vreta), can be dated by stratified finds to the Roman period; it was fully developed at that time with a flat bottom of strakes placed between longitudinally split dugouts. Some years earlier, in 1967 Louwe Kooijmans (State Museum of Antiquities, Leiden) excavated the bottom of a barge,

originally between 35 and 40 m long, radiocarbon-dated to AD 130 ± 30 (Vogel & Waterbolk 1972, 100) and not AD 150 ± 35 (Ellmers 1969, 121; 1972, 292; de Weerd 1977). Marsden (1976; 1977) is correct on this point.

Vessels of the Zwammerdam 'type' are a separate group of Rhine transport ships, used upstream as far as Switzerland (Yverdon and Bevaix: Arnold 1974; 1975; and this volume; Egloff 1974; Ellmers 1974; 1975; Weidmann & Kaenel 1974; possibly also Avenches: Bögli 1974), and within the tradition of Celtic shipbuilding, or rather 'continental' to use a neutral term proposed by Ellmers, Marsden, Arnold, and the present author. General 'Celtic' features are: edge-to-edge planking, the absence of mortise-and-tenon joints, and clenched iron nails for fastening the ribs to the bottom. The continental river barge is typologically connected with the dugout. Its chines are dugouts split longitudinally, or rather hollowed-out trees. To make the sides, the vertical part of such a chine is heightened by one plank (the dugout chines of barge 1 at Pommeroeul (De Boe & Hubert 1976; 1977, 26-31) are not heightened). The system of placing the ribs reflects the intention to adapt the long and narrow, flat-bottomed low-freeboard boat to the conditions of river transport; the alternate placing of the knee- or fork-ended ribs increases transverse stiffening but leaves the longitudinal flexibility unimpaired.

Some details of a ferry-like barge (no 6) reflect the influence of a Mediterranean shipbuilding tradition, as does the steering oar, the sides of which are fastened to the central blade with the mortise-and-tenon joints; its allocation to a specific ship cannot be proven. Some loose planking of coniferous wood retains the Mediterranean

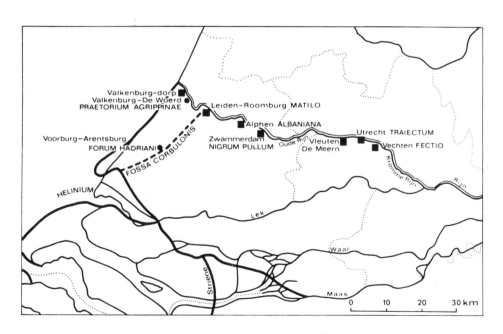

Fig 17   Western part of central Netherlands, with Roman forts on the south bank of the Oude Rijn and hypothetical coastline. Latin names from Peutinger Table (from Bogaers 1971, 129)

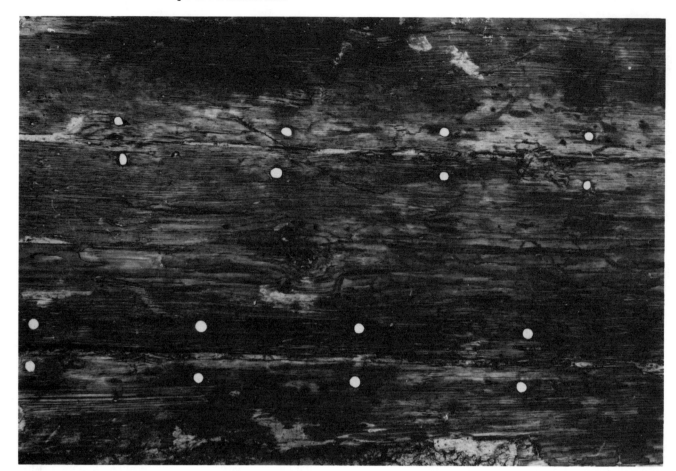

Fig 18   Loose planking with mortise-and-tenon joints; the tenons are emphasized on the photograph (photo IPP: F Gijbels)

mortises and tenons (Fig 18) and so it may be a fragment of a third ship north of the Alps of full Mediterranean construction, along with the County Hall (Marsden 1974) and the Vechten (Muller 1895) boats.

Pollen analysis of the caulking revealed some evidence which points to southern Germany as the region where these barges were built (cf also Druten: Groenman-van Waateringe 1974), as does the wood of the raising of dugout 3 and the deck of dugout 5 (*Abies alba*).

The barges at Zwammerdam, Kapel Avezaath (Louwe Kooijmans 1968), and Druten (Hulst & Lehmann 1974) only came into use after AD 150, a period of trouble with German tribes outside the *limes* of Lower Germany. The Roman military administration needed a transport system to bring stone for rebuilding the old wooden forts downstream. To this end the local south German shipbuilders enlarged their small ships (dugouts, broadened by some planking: Fig 19) up to the size needed by the Roman army. *Provincial* Roman ship-building is a romanization of local pre-Roman traditions: the construction is native in origin, but the size is in fact Roman.

The dugouts
Zwammerdam 1
Cut from an oak tree. Length 6.99 m, width c 1.05 m. Straight stem with hole for anchor post. A vertical timber is nailed to the stern. The three deck planks were fastened to transverse deck beams with iron nails and wooden pegs. A rectangular opening was sawn in the deck and the sides were perforated to let the water in to keep live fish: a fishing boat (section in Fig 19a).

Zwammerdam 5
Construction as for no 1. Length 5.48 m, width 0.76 m. On the deck (of *Abies alba*) a hatch with iron hinges was still movable. The sides were perforated: a fishing boat.

Zwammerdam 3
Cut from an oak tree, trough-shaped in section (Fig 20). Length 10.40 m, width c 1.40 m. Sides raised with an *Abies alba* plank. The stem (with hole) is a separate piece of oak, adzed differently and fastened to the tree with iron nails. Cracks in the dugout tree were repaired before the ribs were placed in position. The ribs were fastened to the tree and the heightened sides with iron nails. There is a small maststep. The system of placing the ribs, in pairs and in alternate positions, resembles the principle used in the barges (Fig 19b).

The barges
Zwammerdam 2
(Fig 21; section in Fig 19c). Length 22.75 m, max width (on bottom) 2.80 m, max height 0.95 m; 37 ribs, fork-ended, placed in alternate positions. Seven strakes, max 15 m in length, 0.35 m wide and 0.08 m thick. Height of

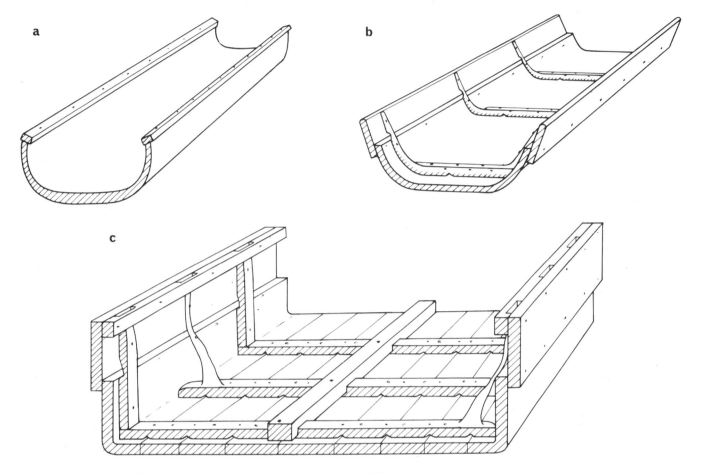

Fig 19   Sections of (a) the simple dugout Zwammerdam 1, (b) the heightened dugout Zwammerdam 3, and (c) the barge Zwammerdam 2. A single dugout can be heightened, and a heightened dugout can be longitudinally split with the intention of placing strakes between the resulting dugout chines (drawings IPP: B Donker)

the starboard side of the L-shaped chine 0.5 m, raised by one plank. Separate uprights slotted into the smooth ends of the ribs. An inner timber is fitted at the top of the side-plank with prefabricated rectangular holes, irrespective of the thick ends of the uprights and the thin ends of the forks of the ribs. Maststep, too small for sailing, at one-quarter distance from the stem; possibly for a towing post. All fastenings are made of large iron nails, partly clenched, and some wooden treenails (rib/strake), as in the supposed native pre-Roman prototypes. In plan the middle part of the ship is rectangular.

Zwammerdam 4

(Fig 22). Length 34 m, max width (on bottom) 4.40 m, max height 1.20 m; 93 ribs, knee-ended, were placed in pairs and in alternate positions. Six strakes, max 21.60 m in length, 0.85 m wide and 0.10 m thick. The ship was distorted by 6 m of sediment and excavation was only possible with the aid of a coffer-dam (State Service for Polder Reclamation). Height of the port side of the L-shaped chine max 0.85 m. Largest plank (chine) *c* 22.40 m in length, 0.10 m thick, 0.85 m in height, bottom part of the chine 0.25 m in width. Chine heightened by one plank. Knee-ends of the ribs and some loose uprights nailed to or inserted in the inner timber at the top of the side-board. One row of stringers nailed to the knees and the uprights. Large maststep for sailing, with additional constructional features, at one-quarter distance from the stem. All fastenings are made of large iron nails, partly clenched. In plan the middle part of the ship is rectangular.

Zwammerdam 6

(Fig 23). Length 20.25 m, max width (on bottom) 3.40 m, max height 0.90 m. Seven strakes, of max shiplength, 0.45 m wide and 0.06 m thick. 30 ribs, knee-ended, were placed in alternate positions. Near the stem and stern two crossed ribs were placed. Near the stem four transverse ribs, fastened on top of the board with swallow-tail. Height of the starboard side of the L-shaped chine 0.45 m. Chine heightened edge-*on*-edge with one plank (0.24 m). Knees inserted in, or enlarged to do so, inner timber on top of the board. Between the flat bottom and stem or stern respectively, a scarfed plank allows the stem and the stern to slope considerably. Excellent-quality nailing and joinery. In two places a mortise-and-tenon joint was used in addition to nails for fastening the timber on edge of the vertical part of the chine (borrowing 'Mediterranean' techniques?). Maststep at one-quarter distance from the stem. All fastenings are made with large iron nails, partly clenched. In plan the ship is gently curved. Stem and stern are, respectively, 2.40 and 2.20 m wide. With iron corner strengthening, this points to function as a ferry-boat.

The steering oar

(Fig 24). Oak. Length 5.15 m, length of the loom 2.80 m, width of the blade 1.24 m. The central part of the blade and the loom are of one piece of wood; two or three holes in the central part of the blade were to fasten it to a ship. A rectangular hole at the top of the loom was to hold a

Fig 20   The heightened dugout Zwammerdam 3 (photo IPP: F Gijbels)

Fig 21   Barge Zwammerdam 2: starboard side. Fork-ended ribs are placed in alternate positions; the uprights
are slotted into the smooth ends of these ribs (photo IPP: F Gijbels)

Fig 22   Barge Zwammerdam 4: part of the bottom and port side. Knee-ended ribs are placed in pairs and in alternate positions. In addition to the knees some separate uprights (photo IPP: F Gijbels)

Fig 23   Ferry-like barge Zwammerdam 6: part of the bottom and a side. Knee-ended ribs are placed in alternate positions. A double-hooked plank is used to brace the rising end-sections (photo IPP: G Verkuil)

Fig 24   Zwammerdam: steering oar. Photograph taken obliquely in situ (photo IPP: G Verkuil)

tiller. The blade is widened by two pieces, fastened to the central part with mortise-and-tenon joints, and at three of the four corners with an iron nail. This shows Mediterranean influence, but parallels are extremely rare. The only example with mortise-and-tenon joints is from the first Lake Nemi ship, other parallels (Housesteads, Bevaix) being cut from a single piece of wood.

The Zwammerdam barges: a type?

Marsden (1976, 44; 1977, 284-5) considers the barges of Zwammerdam to be a special group, but some years earlier Ellmers (1973, 25-30) had considered such barges as an evolutionary stage in the 'alpenländisch-rheinländische Gruppe' (Ellmers 1969, 84-91). The present author produced a rough indication of barge-typology in 1973 (de Weerd & Haalebos 1973, 396-7; see also de Weerd 1976). Along with the 'Zwammerdam' barge type, ranging into the early medieval period, Marsden (1976) considers the 'Blackfriars' type, the 'New Guy's House' type, and the 'Utrecht' type (which might include the heightened dugout Zwammerdam 3) all as belonging to the same family: Celtic shipbuilding (Ellmers 1969: Keltischer Schiffbau). Now, Pommeroeul enters the Zwammerdam group (De Boe & Hubert 1976; 1977) as does Abbeville (Marsden 1977, 284). Marsden (1977, 283) prefers to write 'celtic' and not 'Celtic', the four shipbuilding traditions being only loosely connected with the notion of Celtic tribes, whose territory only partially covers the geographical distribution of Marsden's celtic vessels. Whatever 'celtic' or 'continental' (including the British Isles) may be taken to mean, the main type criteria are: (a) they are geographically neither Mediterranean nor Scandinavian, and (b) some important constructional features from these regions are absent. Type consistency by sharing absent characteristics?

As Zwammerdam 6 confronts us with a rather complex interweaving of 'continental' and 'Mediterranean' technologies, function (at Zwammerdam the river transport of heavy cargoes) should predominate over constructional design, when typological connections are to be clarified. In this way the 'Zwammerdam' type (or group) implies one functional design at the level of actual boatbuilding; any differences between the barges (Zwammerdam, Kapel Avezaath, Druten, Abbeville, Pommeroeul, Yverdon, and Bevaix) are technical

adaptations—in terms of available material, technical equipment, and craftsmanship—designed to carry heavy cargoes downstream and through the natural waterways. In this sense differences between types are only of importance when related to function (ie whether seagoing or river craft), and single technical elements (eg clenched nails) can be used in individual vessels which belong to quite different types. Constructional differences or combinations—mortise-and-tenon, pegging, slotting edge-to-edge, clinker, clenched and other nails, L-shaped or rounded (Druten) chine with (Zwammerdam) or without (Pommeroeul) raised sides—tell us something about the technical skill of the boat-builder and his receptiveness to innovations at the interfaces between different cultures. A number M of different constructional principles is needed to build a vessel, but the boat-builder is acquainted with a greater number N of such principles and makes a choice M out of N, specified for each individual vessel, as opposed to other differing selections M out of the same N; this N is type-consistent. N minus M creates the opportunity for variability in construction across functional and environmental types. Some characteristics are related to the variability of others. It can be easily explained why the vertical sides of the chines in, for example, the Zwammerdam barges are raised and those of Pommeroeul are not. In the Zwammerdam barges the draught is only shallow in relation to the length of the barges; the available height of the long part of the L, shaped from an oak tree, was large, but nevertheless too shallow for the purpose. Even large oak trees did not grow any larger. At Pommeroeul, the length of barge 1 was between 18 and 20 m, and the 'natural' size of the L-shaped oak-tree chine was evidently large enough to obtain the barge's required draught (0.67 m), which is lower than that required at Zwammerdam. It may therefore be supposed that on the barges at Kapel Avezaath and Druten, where the actual construction of the sides is unknown, the L-shaped chines had been raised originally because of their length (Kapel Avezaath: between 35 and 40 m; Druten: c 27 m).

Marsden (1976, 46) considers the Zwammerdam barges to be 'very primitive' because of their dugout chines and (1977, 281) regards the size of these barges as inconsistent with this 'primitive' construction. I do not agree that they are 'primitive', not because I am working on Zwammerdam, but because a typological series (dugout → complicated ship) is not in itself evolutionary in a Darwinian sense. Similarly, a long series of identical technical items in a single artefact 'seems' primitive because of their continual repetition. The impressive size of the Zwammerdam barges 'looks' too big for only a handful of constructional principles. I might reply that a new building design for large vessels with only a small number of traditional techniques sounds rather 'sophisticated' because of the principle of repetition, the aurora of industrial engineering: a Roman Imperial enterprise flying far beyond the Darwinian concept of primitiveness.

References

Arnold, B, 1974   La barque gallo-romaine de la Baie de Bevaix (Lac de Neuchâtel, Suisse), *Cahiers d'archéologie subaquatique* **3**, 133-50.

——, 1975   The Gallo-Roman boat from the Bay of Bevaix, Lake Neuchâtel, Switzerland, *Int J Naut Archaeol Underwater Explor*, **4**, 123-6.

Boe, G De & Hubert, F, 1976   Binnenhafen und Schiffe der Römerzeit von Pommeroeul im Hennegau (Belgien), *Archäologisches Korrespondenzblatt*, **6**, H 3, 227-34.

——, 1977   Une installation portuaire d'époque romaine à Pommeroeul, *Archaeologia Belgica*, **192.**

Bogaers, J E, 1971   in *Oudheidkundige Mededelingen uit het Rijksmuseum van Oudheden te Leiden*, **52.**

Bögli, H, 1974   Vestige d'une embarcation romaine à Avenches, *Helvetia Archaeologia*, **19/20,** 92-3.

Egloff, M, 1974   La barque de Bevaix, épave gallo-romaine du Lac de Neuchâtel, *ibid,* 82-91.

Ellmers, D, 1969   Keltischer Schiffbau, *Jahrbuch des Römisch-Germanischen Zentralmuseums*, **16,** 73-122 (publ 1971).

——, 1972   *Frühmittelalterliche Handelsschiffahrt in Mittel- und Nordeuropa, Offa-Bücher,* **28;** *Schriftenreihe des Deutschen Schiffahrtmuseums Bremerhaven,* **3:** Neumünster.

——, 1973   Rheinschiffe der Römerzeit, *Beiträge zur Rheinkunde,* **25,** 25-41.

——, 1974   Vor- und frühgeschichtliche Schiffahrt am Nordrand der Alpen, *Helvetia Archaeologica,* **19/20,** 94-104.

——, 1975   Reconstitution de la barque gallo-romaine trouvée à Yverdon et datée de la seconde moitié du premier siècle de notre ère, *Eburodunum,* **1,** 165-72, (*Recueil de travaux publiés par l'Institut d'Archéologie Yverdonnoise*).

Groenman-van Waateringe, W, 1974   Analysis of the 'Caulking' from the Roman barge at Druten, Appendix to Hulst & Lehmann 1974, 21-3 (publ 1976).

Haalebos, J K, 1973   *De romeinse castella te Zwammerdam ZH*, thesis, Univ Amsterdam.

——, 1977   *Zwammerdam Nigrum Pullum. Ein Auxiliarkastell am Niedergermanischen Limes, Cingula,* **3:** Amsterdam.

Hulst, R S, & Lehmann, L Th, 1974   The Roman barge of Druten, *Berichten Rijksdienst Oudheidkundig Bodemonderz,* **24,** 7-24 (publ 1976).

Jong, J de, 1977   Conservation of old waterlogged wood, in *Sources and techniques in boat archaeology* (ed Sean McGrail), BAR Supp Ser, **29,** 23-44.

Louwe Kooijmans, L P, 1968   Een onderzoek en een opgraving, *Studium Generale,* **14,** 11, 6-7.

Marsden, P, 1974   The County Hall ship, London, *Int J Naut Archaeol Underwater Explor,* **3,** 55-65.

——, 1976   A boat of the Roman period found at Bruges, Belgium, in 1899, and related types, *ibid,* **5,** 23-55.

——, 1977   Celtic ships of Europe, in *Sources and techniques in boat archaeology* (ed Sean McGrail), BAR Supp Ser, **29,** 281-8.

Muller, Fz, S, 1895   Verslag van de opgravingen van Romeinsche oudheden te Vechten gedaan op kosten van het Provinciaal Utrechts Genootschap van Kunsten en Wetenschappen in de jaren 1892-1894, *Verslag van het verhandelde in de Algemeene Vergadering van het Provinciaal Utrechts Genootschap van Kunsten en Wetenschappen,* gehouden den 25 Juni 1895, spec 129-42, 160-1, Pl IV & V.

Vogel, J C, & Waterbolk, H T, 1972   Groningen radiocarbon dates X, *Radiocarbon,* **14,** 1, 6-110.

Weerd, M D de, 1976   Schepen in de Romeinse tijd naar Zwammerdam (ZH), *Westerheem,* **25,** 129-37 (*Polonaise der pre- en protohistorie,* 62-70).

——, 1977   Römerzeitliche Transportschiffe und Einbäume aus Nigrum Pullum/Zwammerdam (Z.-H.), *Studien zu den Militärgrenzen Roms II,* 187-98, Taf 13-19 (Vorträge des 10. internationalen Limeskongresses in der Germania Inferior), Beihèft 38 der *Bonner Jahrbücher.*

Weerd, M D de, & Haalebos, J K, 1973   Schepen voor het opscheppen, *Spiegel Historiael,* **8,** 386-97.

Weidmann, D, & Kaenel, G, 1974   La barque romaine d'Yverdon, *Helvetia Archaeologica,* **19/20,** 66-81.

Roman boats from a small river harbour at Pommeroeul, Belgium   Guy De Boe

At the end of July 1975, the digging of a new canal in the territory of Pommeroeul, a small village lying near the French border nearly halfway between Mons and Tournai (Fig 25), led to the discovery of an archaeological site of exceptional interest. Numerous finds, timber structures, and part of a dugout seemed to belong to a previously unknown Roman village. The site is located on the Roman road leading from Bavai to the north, at the point where this road crosses the junction of the river Haine and a small tributary, both entirely silted up since the beginning of the 19th century.

The archaeological remains in this area can be divided into three sectors (Fig 26):

i The tributary of the river Haine. A rescue excavation organized by the Service national des Fouilles from August to October 1975, directed by F Hubert and the author, resulted in the discovery of numerous finds from the late Bronze Age to the late Iron Age, including the decades immediately following the Roman conquest, and the excavation of a small Roman harbour and five boats. Only the latter will be presented here: the full interim report is by De Boe and Hubert (1977).

ii The river Haine itself, cut through by canal works in the early months of 1976. No rescue excavation or even small investigations were allowed. According to information, mostly supplied reluctantly by amateurs and treasure hunters, the river bed also produced numerous finds, including a timber-built quay, consolidated with stones, and at least one boat, a dugout canoe measuring some 15 m in length and almost completely filled with pottery.

iii The village, occupying most of the area between the two rivers. Building remains, in timber as well as in masonry, were located on both sides of the Roman road. No excavation could be carried out before they were covered up by several metres of earth from the new canal. This village was apparently inhabited between about AD 30-40 and the second half of the 3rd century.

Along the tributary of the Haine, an area of about 3 ha was examined, starting at a depth of 2.50 m below the present ground level, the most important parts being excavated. The main river bed showed remains of bank revetments consisting of constantly renewed rows of piles driven into the silt and the bank. The harbour itself was constructed in a narrow side-branch, about 16-17 m wide and separated from the main river by a small island.

Like the main bed, this side-branch consisted of several consecutive channels. Apparently, it ran first along the island, moved to the north-east, eroding the older silts containing the pre-Roman material, and then turned back again to the centre in successive stages. Following this movement of the channel, the bank revetments or quays were repeatedly renewed, but always constructed against the north-eastern bank. The analysis of the best preserved quay, although it had been reduced to a disorderly heap of timber, mostly oak, permitted its reconstruction as follows. It consisted of planking, at least six courses high, shored vertically against the bank by a row of piles, driven into the bottom of the channel through the previously deposited silt. This quay was not anchored into the bank as was the one discovered in Xanten (von Petrikovits 1952). It could not resist the earth pressure and, when the bank collapsed, the piles crashed downwards (Fig 27).

The most important construction in this small harbour is the most recent, dating from the 2nd century AD, probably the second half. It is a large platform, measuring about 15 m in length and 6-7 m in wide (Fig 28). The oak planks, about 30 mm thick, were simply laid down or nailed to eight heavy cross-beams. Since this platform sagged some 0.5-0.6 m, the binding between these beams and the heavy piles was not preserved. The piles were only eleven in number. It therefore seems probable that the ends of the beams were partly resting on the bank and partly supported by the piles. The exact function of this strong oak construction is difficult to define, because it lay right in the middle of the channel. From analysis of the sections it seems probable that access of boats to the quay became impossible because of accumulation of silt against it, and that this construction was a landing stage, built in the partly silted channel to avoid the muddy banks.

Four of the five boats were abandoned on either side of the channel during the second half of the 1st or the early 2nd century AD. They were rapidly covered by the silt deposited under the later landing stage and against the banks. The fifth boat seems to have been abandoned in the second half of the 2nd or early 3rd century and lay almost in the middle, on the bottom of the channel. These dates are still provisional and must be confirmed by a complete analysis of the finds and by radiocarbon and dendrochronological dating.

One wreck was too badly destroyed to allow an identification of its type. Only two planks and two fragments of ribs were preserved over a total length of 4.40 m and a width of 1 m. They showed several repairs

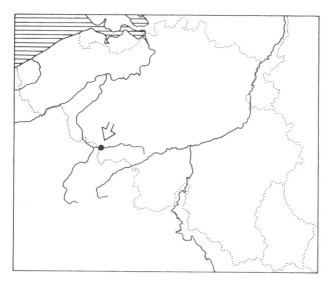

Fig 25   Location of Pommeroeul, Belgium

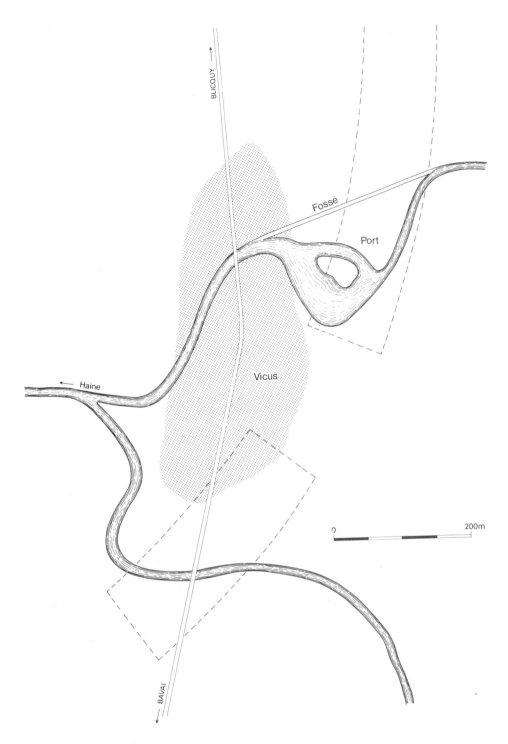

Fig 26　General plan of the site in the Roman period

with small iron plates nailed over the cracks. The four others belong to two different boat types which are only suitable for inland navigation: the dugout canoe and the larger flat-bottomed barge, both keel-less. They provide interesting information on shipbuilding in the 'Celtic' tradition, which is clearly distinct from the Scandinavian and classical Mediterranean shipbuilding methods (Marsden 1976; Ellmers 1969).

The first canoe was discovered by an amateur archaeologist, Mr L Demarez, before the author's excavations started. No detailed information about it is available. A sketch and approximate section were drawn from newspaper photographs (Fig 29). They show part of a dugout, about 1 m in breadth and preserved over a length of some 4 m. The almost vertical sides are heightened by an additional strake, which overlapped

Fig 27   The remains of a collapsed and crushed quay

Fig 28   The 'landing stage'

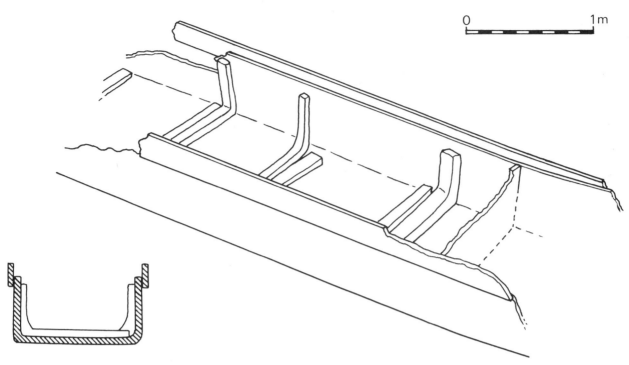

Fig 29   Sketch and approximate section of the first dugout canoe

and was nailed to the upper edge of the dugout. The hull is consolidated by several pairs of L-shaped ribs, the knees of which are disposed head to tail. A transverse plank may belong to a partition.

The second canoe, probably some 11.50-12 m long, is preserved over a length of 9.70 m. It is 0.98 m wide and only 0.58 m high, including the gunwale. The hull, of oak, is about 50 mm thick (Fig 30). The construction of this carvel-built boat is based on the traditional dugout canoe, improved by additional planks and a separately built prow or stern. The central part, over 7 m long, is almost entirely made from a single dugout trunk, the outer rounding of which is preserved on the sides. Only the bottom is flattened. Three major planks are inserted in this dugout. Two of them, with rounded and scarfed joints, face each other under both sides. The third, which is long and narrow, is inserted in the lower part of one side. They are fixed with long iron nails, driven right into the edge of the planks, or obliquely into small hollows. This part of the hull is consolidated by only two pairs of light L-shaped ribs, as usual arranged head to tail and fixed by nails. A fifth rib is cut within the hull from the mass of the trunk.

The prow or stern—no distinction is possible—is composed of three elements: a central plank, with its pointed end inserted into the bottom of the dugout, between two symmetrical L-shaped side-planks. These bilge-strakes, which extend to the full height of the sides and are fixed to the central dugout by long oblique scarfed joints, are spoon-shaped, to form a slender prow: the bottom rises to the full height of the gunwale and the slightly incurved sides end in a point. The extremity is covered by a small rectangular platform of 320 × 520 mm, against which abut the semicircular pinewood caps running along both gunwales. All these elements are also fixed by iron nails and two straight ribs.

The use of the L-shaped bilge-strakes, typical of the flat-bottomed river barges of the Zwammerdam type, is probably limited here to the two ends. Although this

might only be an application of an already developed technique to strengthen the weakest parts of the dugout, the rising prow and stern, this craft could be considered as an interesting transitional form between the traditional dugout and the larger barges of the Zwammerdam type. It has indeed been suggested that the L-shaped bilge-strakes of these barges originated from a dugout split longitudinally, in other words by extending to the whole craft what is here limited to the ends. This is very clearly shown by the first barge from Pommeroeul.

Of this barge, which may have been at least 18-20 m long, only part of the midship section and the stern were preserved over a length of 12.70 m (Fig 31). It was almost 3 m wide and 0.67 m high, including the gunwale. The oak planks are about 60 mm thick. Putting the L-shaped sides of this craft together one obtains exactly the same section as in the canoe just described. It therefore seems almost certain that the starting point of the construction was a dugout canoe, which was split longitudinally. The half-dugouts were separated and the bottom enlarged by inserting planks. By contrast with similar barges found at Yverdon (Weidmann & Kaenel 1974; Ellmers 1975) and Bevaix (Egloff 1974; Arnold 1974) in Switzerland, and at Zwammerdam (de Weerd and Haalebos 1973; de Weerd 1976) and Druten (Hulst & Lehmann 1974) in the Netherlands, the sides are not heightened by an additional strake. In a third stage, the carvel-built hull has been consolidated by ribs.

Apart from a few small filling pieces, only three planks were inserted between the two half-dugouts in the long flat bottom of the midship section, prolonged by four shorter ones in the rising bottom of the stern. With one exception, they are joined obliquely, forming a scarfed joint. A few saw-toothed grooves are only superficial. These planks are not nailed to one another.

As in the preceding canoe, each side of this barge was also composed of probably three elements in a row and nailed together with long oblique scarfed joints: a long

Fig 31   The first barge

Fig 30   The second canoe

Fig 32   The gangplank of the first barge

straight half-dugout over the whole length of the flat-bottomed midship section, a shorter half-dugout at the rising stern, and probably a similar one at the prow. The half-dugouts at the stern are spoon-shaped, with rising bottoms and slightly incurved sides. As on the other boats, caulking consisted of cord, fixed between the planks by a large number of small nails, mostly spaced at close intervals. No traces of laths have been observed.

The cohesion of the hull was assured by a large number of L-shaped ribs, as usual laid in pairs, in one case in a group of three, arranged head to tail and with their knees supporting the sides. These ribs were fixed by iron nails, driven from above as well as from below, into the bottom planks, and only from the inside into the sides; projecting points were clenched.

Near the stern, the starboard side was preserved to its full height. Four elements make up the gunwale, all of them fixed with iron nails (Fig 32). First, a beam was laid longitudinally on the upper edge of the half-dugout. A plank was fixed against it on the inside, resting on the knees of the ribs. Both these elements supported the horizontal gunwale, a 220 mm wide plank provided with an inner rim and transverse ridges. Finally, a fourth plank was fixed on the outside against the gunwale. This particular construction seems to be related to the way in which this craft was propelled. Although it may well have been equipped for sailing on larger waters and for towing, it would surely have been poled on small and meandering rivers with marshy banks, such as the Haine. The presence of a gangplank on the gunwale, provided with ridges to prevent slipping, made it possible for the boatmen handling the poles to move from stem to stern without being hindered by the cargo packed in the bottom. The outer plank was to prevent damage to the hull while manoeuvring with the poles.

A cabin occupied the stern over a length of 2.30 m, with behind it a poop of about 1.80 m.* Its walls were made from very thin overlapping oak planks on the outside and thicker pinewood planks on the inside. These were nailed on light posts fixed into mortises cut into the bottom ribs and the gangplank. The roof was further supported by a central post which was also fixed to a rib. Inside the cabin, the floor was made level by laying pinewood planks between the ribs and covering them with an organic material, probably straw.

The second barge lay stranded on the slope of the channel. Only the lower side and part of the bottom were preserved in two pieces, over a total length of about 15 m. Without gunwale, the side was only 0.5 m high and the oak planks were about 50-60 mm thick. Built according to the same principles, this craft, however,

---

*The oldest previously known archaeological evidence for the existence of a cabin dates from about 1400: the Kogge of Bremen and the ship of Maytham (Ellmers 1972).

Fig 33   The rising end of the second barge

Fig 34   Different forms of pole ferrules and boathooks

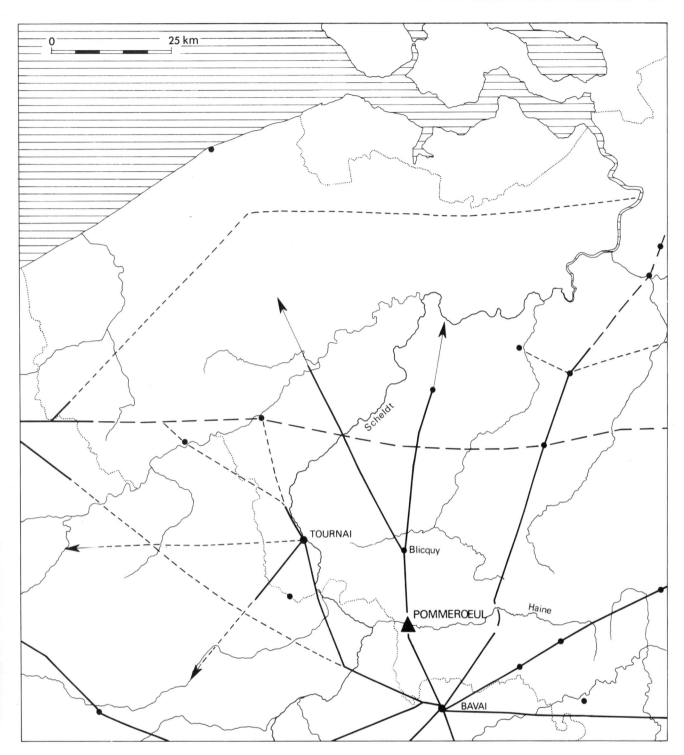

Fig 35   Location of Pommeroeul in the network of water-routes and Roman roads in western Belgium (after a map by J Mertens)

shows a few differences in construction. The bottom planks are nailed to one another, and so the hull was stronger and needed only a small number of ribs. The half dugout did not reach the full height of the sides and was partly heightened by an additional plank. At the only preserved rising end, the side consists not of a spoon-shaped half-dugout, but of several smaller pieces assembled edge-to-edge or at right-angles (Fig 33).

From the very large quantity of finds recovered from the river silts, special mention should be made of those related to shipping: several dozen pole ferrules and boathooks of different shapes (Fig 34), anchor stones or weights for fishing-nets, and a possible sounding lead, also made of stone, with a groove for a string. Others provide information about domestic and economic activities in the village and in the neighbourhood of the river, such as woodworking, agriculture, tanning, and leather manufacture, and about the types of freight which were shipped from here: leather, peat, coal, building materials from nearby quarries, pottery, and probably agricultural produce from the many villas spread over the countryside.

Trade from and to the Roman village of Pommeroeul was certainly favoured by its situation at the intersection of two routes (Fig 35). By land, Pommeroeul was connected to the coastal area and, via near-by Bavai, to the whole network of roads in northern Gaul. By water, the shallow-draught vessels could certainly go much farther up the river, collecting the produce of this fertile land. Downstream, the current slowly carried the boats to the Scheldt and, northwards, to the mouths of the Meuse and the Rhine.

References

Arnold, B, 1974   La barque gallo-romaine de la Baie de Bevaix, *Cahiers d'archéologie subaquatique*, **3**, 133-50.

Boe, G De, & Hubert, F, 1977   Une installation portuaire d'époque romaine à Pommeroeul, *Archaeologia Belgica*, **192.**

Egloff, M, 1974   La barque de Bevaix, épave gallo-romaine du Lac de Neuchâtel, *Helvetia Archaeologica*, **19/20,** 82-91.

Ellmers, D, 1969   Keltischer Schiffbau, *Jahrbuch des Römisch-Germanischen Zentralmuseums Mainz*, **16,** 73-122.

——, 1972   *Frühmittelalterliche Handelsschiffahrt in Mittel- und Nordeuropa, Offa-Bücher,* **28.**

——, 1975   Reconstitution de la barque gallo-romaine trouvée à Yverdon, *Eburodunum*, **1,** 167-72.

Hulst, R S, & Lehmann, L Th, 1974   The Roman barge of Druten, *Berichten Rijksdienst Oudheidkundig Bodemonderz*, **24,** 7-24.

Marsden, P, 1976   A boat of the Roman period found at Bruges, Belgium, in 1899, and related types, *Int J Naut Archaeol Underwater Explor*, **5,** 23-55.

Petrikovits, H von, 1952   Die Ausgrabungen in der Colonia Traiana bei Xanten, *Bonner Jahrbücher*, **152,** 138ff.

Weerd, M D de, 1976   Schepen in de Romeinse tijd naar Zwammerdam (ZH), *Westerheem*, **25,** 129-37.

Weerd, M D de, & Haalebos, J K, 1973   Schepen voor het opscheppen, *Spiegel Historiael*, **8,** 386-97.

Weidmann, D, & Kaenel, G, 1974   La barque romaine d'Yverdon, *Helvetia Archaeologica*, **19/20,** 66-81.

The lakes of Neuchâtel, Morat, and Bienne (Biel) are situated at about the same altitude and form a homogeneous hydrographic whole.

This area is rich in remains of river navigation, as evidenced by the discovery of the Bevaix and Yverdon boats and the revealing, as a result of preliminary excavations, of traces of the wharf at the Roman port of Avenches. This town is situated on Lake Morat and was constructed with stone from the quarries of Hauterive and La Lance (Concise). These quarries were located on Lake Neuchâtel. In the La Lance quarry traces of ancient exploitation can still be discerned.

Of the five recorded inscriptions relating to shipping in Switzerland, four were found at Geneva and Lausanne. They draw attention to the presence of the *nautae* of Lake Geneva or Lake Léman (*lacus Lemanni* or *Lemanno*) and of the *ratiariorum superiorum*. The fifth inscription was discovered at Avenches and refers to the *nautae Aruranci Aramici* (Howald & Meyer 1940: Geneva nos 92 and 108, Lausanne nos 152 and 154, Avenches no 217; for *Aramici* see pp 374-7).

The importance of navigation on Lake Geneva, demonstrated by these inscriptions, is further confirmed by the discovery of the Geneva and Lausanne-Vidy harbours.

The Celtic boats

It is only very recently that a new tradition of boat construction, demonstrated by Ellmers (1969), has been confirmed with the aid of the following discoveries: New Guy's House (1958) and Blackfriars 1 (1962) in England; Kapel Avezaath (1968) and Zwammerdam 2,4,6 (1972-75) in Holland; Bruges (1899; cf also Marsden 1976) and Pommeroeul (1975) in Belgium; and finally Bevaix (1970-73) and Yverdon (1971-72) in Switzerland.

This tradition is located geographically between the Mediterranean region (carvel planking held together edgeways by mortise-and-tenon joints) and Scandinavia where coastal boat building reached its height during the Viking period, with its marvellous clinker-built boats, such as those from Oseberg, Gokstad, Skuldelev, etc.

Essentially this new building tradition covers the inland waters of Europe and the northern coast. The Lake Neuchâtel boats give a new dimension to this region, characterized by carvel-built boats, constructed with thick, broad oak planks. The bottom is flat, without a keel. The bilge-strakes, with their L-shaped section, assure the direct transition of the bottom to the sides of the boat. Frames and planks are fixed with the help of large iron nails often clenched over at right-angles (Figs 36 and 37).

Although all these finds belong to the 1st to 4th centuries AD, the diversity and perfection of this Celtic boat construction (the form changed little until the 20th century) could only be the result of an old tradition handed down from at least the Iron Age, if not from the Bronze Age.

The two Gallo-Roman or Celtic boats of Bevaix and Yverdon are not the only examples of this type of vessel that have been discovered in the three Jura lakes. They have made it possible to identify a fragment of wood discovered in 1973 at Avenches as belonging to a plank. This fragment, 0.8 m long, has a row of caulking nails on one side.

Fig 36   The Bevaix boat lying 2 m below the level of Lake Neuchâtel

Fig 37   The Yverdon boat during the 1971 excavations (after Weidmann & Kaenel 1974)

Caulking and Celtic naval construction

The study of a multiplicity of details will soon make it possible to distinguish several more or less important types of Celtic boat.

For example, the caulking process permits a clear differentiation between the boats discovered in England (caulked with hazel twigs) and those from Lake Neuchâtel (caulked with string covered by a layer of moss which was in turn held by a wooden lath that was secured with thousands of little caulking nails). A detailed study made it possible to specify the observations made on the Yverdon boat (Weidmann & Kaenel 1974, 76) and to verify the absolute similarity between the caulking of the Bevaix and Yverdon boats. The caulking process used on the Rhine delta boats has not yet been published.

Furthermore, study of complex caulking with moss revealed one of the important characteristics of Celtic boat building which has lasted to the present day. For the last half-century it has been confined to a strip north of the Alpine arc, including the lakes of the Salzkammergut, southern Bavaria, the Swiss plateau, northern Savoy, and the region of the Saône.

From a study of present-day caulking, resemblances could be established between regions of the river Aar and Lake Bourget, Lake Neuchâtel, and the Saône (Fig 38).

Similar conclusions will be established when the caulking process used on the Rhine delta boats is published.

A wooden monument

The study of a boat can be carried out from several aspects. It may, for example be studied as an example of boat building, as transport carrier, as a reflection of the importance of trade (economic or political stability resulting in the construction of larger vessels), its cargo can be analysed, and so on.

An aspect that has been little studied is the technology of wood working. Boats are in effect the largest and most complex wooden monuments that have come down to us through the ages. The lake and river environments in which boats are discovered are generally very favourable to the preservation of wood.

Traces of woodworking on a boat are usually well preserved *beneath* the frames (Fig 39). These areas are protected from wear and tear during the use of the boat. On the Bevaix boat it was possible to study the traces left by the pit-saw on the planks and by vigorous axe blows on the frames.

During the construction of a facsimile of the Bevaix maststep it was possible to carry out a detailed study. The growth rings of the tree showed that the maststep

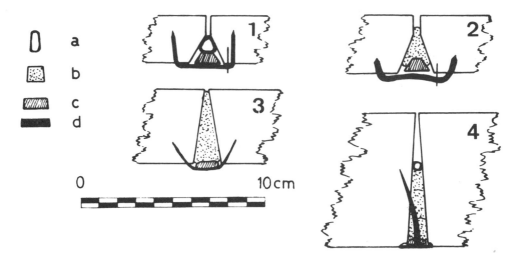

Fig 38   Caulking methods used in the north-western sector of the Alpine arc: 1 Weidling (River Aar, 20th century); 2 senne boat (Lake Bourget, 20th century); 3 nâcon from Cudrefin (Lake Neuchâtel, 19th century); 4 Bevaix and Yverdon boats (Lake Neuchâtel, 1st or 2nd century AD). a=string, b=moss, c=wooden lath, d=iron nail (4) or clamp (1-3)

was not made from an oak trunk stump split down the middle. The two extremities seem to have been cut from a trunk split down the middle, but the centre part is 40-50 mm thicker. Such a piece could not be obtained by splitting the wood, but only by sawing it.

It would also be shown that wood splitting had been replaced by sawing because it was much more economical.

The Bevaix boat

This descriptive chapter is based on four plans, A,B,C,D on Fig 40, which will demonstrate the remarkable construction of this boat.

The Bevaix boat is 19.4 m long, 2.9 m wide (ratio 6.7:1), and 0.9 m high. It is characterized by a flat bottom, without a keel or a central plank. The bottom consists of four large oak planks (1,2,3,4 on Fig 40A), 10.7-12.7 m long, arranged one beside another, each systematically staggered in relation to its neighbour. The first plank forms the stern and the last the prow. A symmetrical

bottom is obtained by adding two planks (5 and 6). The beam was determined by the addition of bilge-strakes; these were L-shaped in section and allowed a direct transition to be made between the flat bottom and the sides of the boat.

In the case of the Bevaix boat the bottom is too long to have a bilge-strake made from a single piece of wood. Two L-shaped elements, overlapping one another, were therefore used for each bilge-strake. Thus the shipwrights were able to overcome the restrictions imposed on the size of the boats by the length of the trees available to them.

Seven puzzling rows of round treenails were arranged perpendicularly to the axis of the four principal bottom planks of the boat, but not to its axis. The treenails are represented on Fig 40 by black crosses.

Driven into holes 0.02 m in diameter, the treenails of silver fir (*Abies alba*) traverse the thickness of the hull. Each row of treenails generally comprises one (occasionally two) per strake and was covered by a pair of frames

Fig 39   Lower face of mast step from Bevaix boat, showing curious traces of working in centre section. Three successive series of scratches in parabola form are recut by axe strokes (top left of picture)

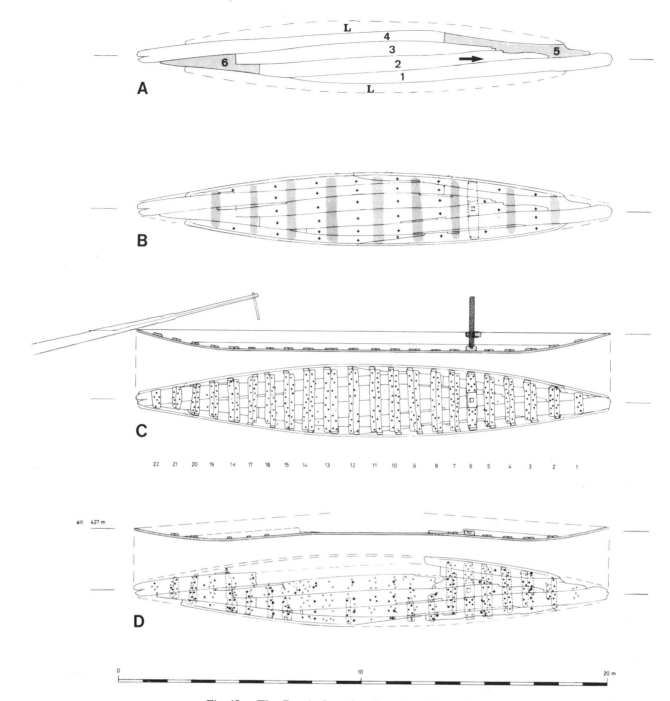

Fig 40   The Bevaix boat (explanations in text)

in the sequence 3,5-6,8,10,12,14,16 and 18. They could, therefore, only have functioned before these pairs of frames were fitted during the building of the vessel.

The following explanation is proposed: once the four planks (1-4) had been placed side by side and slightly staggered in relation to each other, seven transverse rows of holes were drilled. The holes were transfixed by metal rods or long stout treenails, and a system of lashings would have bound each plank to its neighbour at the seven positions. Thus a rigid, tight-fitting bottom was achieved before the pairs of frames, 2,4,7,9,11,13,15,17 and 19, were nailed on. The sequence of frames is represented in grey on Fig 40B.

Subsequently, the lashings were removed and the seven rows of holes were closed with the round fir treenails. The strakes remained tight-fitting, held by the first series

of frames, while the second (3,5-6,8, etc) was fastened over the treenails which lay in the zone in which the frames were to be fitted.

The space between the pairs of frames and the disposition of the frames in each pair is very regular. Thus the upward curving part of the first frame of each pair rose on the starboard side, except for pair 16.

In the present reconstruction of the Bevaix boat the thwart that helps support the mast is based on that discovered on the Zwammerdam boat 4 (Fig 40C). This type of construction was, incidentally, still in current use in Swiss boats at the beginning of the present century.

The connection between the steering-oar and the boat needs further study. The solution to this problem is probably to be found at the level of the frame (or pair of frames) 22.

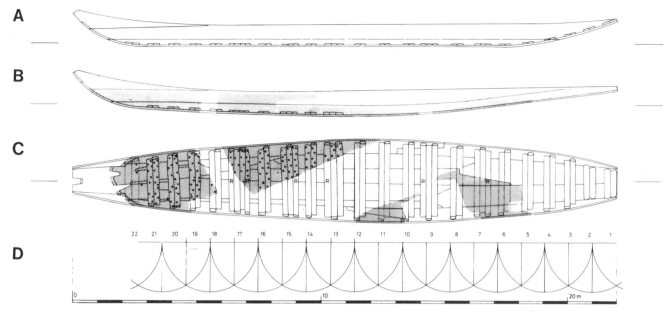

Fig 41   Reconstruction of the Yverdon boat: A most probable profile; B profile based on excavation records; C reconstruction of bottom with surviving elements shown in black; D scale used to show the regular disposition of the series of frames (R=repairs)

The bottom, once solidly assembled, was caulked, and then an end plank was added on each side.

In order better to emphasize the planking structure, the frames still existing have been drawn using a broken line (Fig 40D). The position of nails (●) or of their traces (square-section holes (○)) make it possible to locate the pairs of frames with accuracy.

Likewise, on the basis of the round wooden pegs (+), discussed above, it has been possible to show the presence of square pegs (■). These square pegs show the places where some frames have been replaced. In other cases (eg at Yverdon), the shipwrights have simply added one or two frames to the defective pairs.

Rupture of the connection between the two L-shaped pieces constituting the bilge-strakes had an important consequence in the modification of the longitudinal profile. Yet because of the two well preserved pieces of the bilge-strakes (portside forward and starboard aft), it was relatively easy to obtain the original profile of this boat.

The Yverdon boat

This boat (Figs 37 and 41) was seriously damaged by construction work in 1946 and again in 1971. The fragments that survived this destruction have a total length of 17 m. They nevertheless permit the boat to be described with some accuracy. The length is estimated to have been 20.5-24 m (Ellmers 1974), the width 3.3 m, the height 0.9 m, and the thickness of the planks 0.07-0.1 m. The bottom of the boat, which is preserved, is constructed from an irregular assembly of planks. The transition between the flat bottom and the sides is made by four L-shaped elements.

Analogies between the Bevaix and Yverdon boats are numerous. Perfect similarity can be demonstrated in the complex caulking used between the planks and in the cracks in the planks. The placing of the frames is also very regular and reveals traces of repairs. Such traces can be observed on the 17th row of frames (the first and the last frames were added later), on the 15th (first frame), and on the 13th (last frame). The existence of a hypothetical maststep in the 17th row of frames (Weidmann & Kaenel 1974, 81) may thus be ruled out.

Another element merits attention: the cutting of the planks at the end of the surviving extremity. This structure clearly indicates that elements were added to form important heightening of this extremity. In that position the presence of some nails and especially round- and square-sectioned treenails of various diameters can be observed. If this boat is now compared with the pictorial representations of the river boat on the reverse side of the tombstone of the boatman Blussus and the sailing vessel loaded with amphorae represented on the Oceanus mosaic at Bad Kreuznach (Ellmers 1974), this raised extremity may be interpreted as being the stern.

The extraordinary homogeneity of the main lines of these Celtic boats and at the same time the extraordinary variety in the construction of each vessel are noteworthy.

(*Translated by Jeanny Arnold*)

References

Arnold, B, 1974   La barque gallo-romaine de la Baie de Bevaix, *Cahiers d'archéologie subaquatique*, **3**, 133-50.
——, 1975   The Gallo-Roman boat from the Bay of Bevaix, Lake Neuchâtel, Switzerland, *Int J Naut Archaeol Underwater Explor*, **4**, 123-6.
Egloff, M, 1974   La barque de Bevaix, épave gallo-romaine du lac de Neuchâtel, *Helvetia Archaeologica*, **19/20**, 82-91.
Ellmers, D, 1969   Keltischer Schiffbau, *Jahrbuch des Römisch-Germanischen Zentralmuseums Mainz*, **16**, 73-122.
——, 1974   Vor- und frühgeschichtliche Schiffahrt am Nordrand der Alpen, *Helvetia Archaeologica*, **19/20**, 94-104.
Howald, E, & Meyer, E, 1940   *Die römische Schweiz: Texte und Inschriften mit Uebersetzung.*
Marsden, P, 1976   A boat of the Roman period found at Bruges, Belgium, in 1899, and related types, *Int J Naut Archaeol Underwater Explor*, **5**, 23-55.
Weidmann, D, & Kaenel, G, 1974   La barque romaine d'Yverdon, *Helvetia Archaeologica*, **19/20**, 66-81.

Roman harbours in Britain south of Hadrian's Wall
Henry Cleere

Introduction

A literature search for information about harbours in Roman Britain is an unrewarding exercise. It soon becomes clear that there is virtually no 'hard' evidence, in the form of excavated wharves and jetties, though excavators of Roman civil and military settlements tend to be prodigal with inferred locations for harbour installations. A summary of the scanty evidence available was prepared by Fryer for the 1971 Colston Conference on marine archaeology (Fryer 1973), and it is not proposed to duplicate this survey in the present paper.

Instead, an attempt will be made to examine the likely distribution of ports and harbours in the province, based on what is known of the settlement and trade patterns, and from this to suggest the most promising lines for future investigation.

Before beginning the paper, however, it is necessary to define what is intended by the term 'harbour'. There is considerable imprecision about the use of this and related terms such as wharf, quay, port, jetty etc, which are often used indiscriminately by archaeologists. For the purpose of this study 'harbour' will be taken to apply to any installation from which goods and passengers could be transferred from ship to shore, and vice versa. This will thus encompass man-made constructions, varying in complexity from an elaborate series of stone or wooden wharves and docks down to a simple wooden jetty or revetted river bank, and natural havens—sheltered anchorages from which goods and passengers could be landed by lighters working off an open shore, or where shallow-draught vessels could be safely beached. It is the unquestioned existence of harbours of the latter type, as

evidenced by boat excavations and by the minimum requirements of many Roman boats, that makes the scanty archaeological record an unsatisfactory starting point for a survey of Roman harbours in the context of a conference on Roman shipping and trade.

Evidence from the road system

Fryer begins his survey (1973, 261) by stating, with ample justification, that 'In contrast with what is known of the road system of Roman Britain, our knowledge of the ports of that period is somewhat limited'. However, having thus introduced the notion of the road system, he fails to profit from the opportunity that it offers for the systematic study of likely harbour locations. The Ordnance Survey *Map of Roman Britain* (3rd ed, 1956) indicates the following possible port and harbour sites, where proven roads end at coastal settlements or where settlements are located on navigable rivers of major estuaries (starting at the eastern end of the Wall and travelling clockwise round the coast, as shown in Fig 42):

1	The Tyne estuary	24	Hamworthy
2	Scarborough	25	Radipole
3	Filey	26	Exeter/Topsham
4	York	27	Sea Mills
5	Brough-on-Humber	28	Gloucester
6	Winteringham	29	Caerwent
7	Lincoln	30	Caerleon
8	Brancaster	31	Cardiff
9	Caister-by-Yarmouth	32	Neath
10	Burgh Castle	33	Carmarthen
11	Colchester/Fingringhoe	34	Pennal
12	Bradwell	35	Caernarvon
13	London	36	Caerhûn
14	Rochester	37	Chester
15	Reculver	38	Wilderspool
16	Richborough	39	Ribchester
17	Dover	40	Lancaster
18	Lympne	41	Ravenglass
19	Hastings	42	Moresby
20	Pevensey	43	Maryport
21	Chichester/Fishbourne	44	Beckfoot
22	Portchester	45	Bowness
23	Bitterne		

The list is an impressive one and is, indeed, susceptible to enlargement: there are, for example, apparently isolated sites such as Caer Gybi on Anglesey which are not related to a road system and are thus more likely to have been supplied by sea. In its present form the list is an undifferentiated one; it needs revaluation in the light of what is known of the settlement pattern in the hinterland of these putative harbours and of their raison d'être (ie whether they were primarily civil or military establishments).

Military harbours

Accepting the existence of a generalized Severn-Humber line dividing the military zone from the civil, the sites from the Tyne mouth to the Humber on the east coast and from Caerleon to Bowness on the west coast may be presumed to be military. Only at Wilderspool is there as

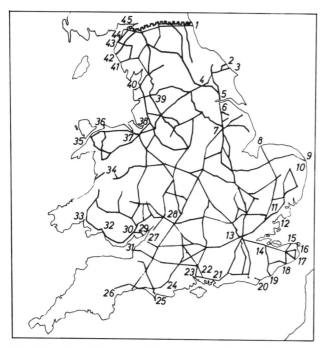

Fig 42   Possible sites of harbours in Roman Britain

yet no clear evidence of any kind of military establishment; recent excavations (Williams 1970; Spencer 1975) have given no indication that the extensive industrial establishment there was founded or run by the army, although it is tempting to see a link with the XX Legion at Chester.

To these northern sites should be added the Saxon Shore (and in some cases earlier *Classis Britannica*) forts on the south-eastern coasts, from Brancaster to Portchester.

The northern defensive system of the Wall and its associated forts and signal stations account for one group of these sites—the mouth of the Tyne and Bowness at opposite ends of the Wall, Scarborough and Filey on the east coast, and Beckfoot, Maryport, Moresby, and Ravenglass on the west. It is clear from the great granaries at South Shields (Richmond 1953) that this was a major supply base, but no harbour installations have been found. However, it now appears that this particular installation was built for a specific purpose (the Severan campaign in Scotland) and operated for only a few years, and so the permanent harbour for the Wall garrisons is probably more likely to be located at the Wallsend fort, where certain indications of wharves have come to light over the years (J P Gillam, pers comm).

The potential harbours associated with the forts along the Cumbrian coast have recently been discussed by Jarrett (1976). He concludes that the major harbour for the garrisons on this coast would have been located at Maryport. The other candidate, Moresby, is just navigable for shallow-draught vessels, but there are dangerous rock outcrops on the lee shore to the prevailing south-westerlies and so landing would have been hazardous. Beckfoot is a completely open shore and so could only have been reached by lighters plying between the fort and vessels standing offshore, and there is no suitable harbour below the magnificent site of Ravenglass.

The eastern sites associated with the Wall at Scarborough and Filey were relatively small signal stations, and the former is located on a clifftop high above the sea. However, the Filey station is situated in a good natural harbour and it is possible that it might have served as an unloading point for supplies destined for the important fort at Malton (although this fort lies equally close to York).

The group of sites between Lancaster and Gloucester has been studied by Livens (1974) in search of a hypothetical '*Litus Hibernicum*', paralleling the Saxon Shore of the south-east. Lancaster itself, at the head of the sheltered Lune estuary, is a very likely site for a substantial harbour installation; it is known from the *Notitia Dignitatum* (Occ xl) that a naval unit, the *numerus barcariorum Tigrisiensium*, was stationed at Olenacum, which has been fairly confidently identified with Lancaster (Frere 1974, 262, n 20) in the late 4th century, which presupposes berthing facilities for warships. The changing shoals of the Lune estuary may well conceal some substantial works.

Chester was, of course, the headquarters of the XX Legion, with a considerable civil settlement alongside. It is located on the Dee estuary, not perhaps the easiest waterway to navigate at the present time, but shoal conditions may have deteriorated since the Roman period. Fryer (1973, 246-7, fig 2) discusses the remains of early wharves that have come to light both at Chester and at the nearby Heronbridge settlement, and also considers the significance of finds of Flintshire lead and north

Wales slate in terms of trade. It is certain that the large military and civil settlements at Chester would have required extensive wharfing facilities.

The auxiliary forts at Caerhûn, Caernarvon, Pennal, Carmarthen, Neath, and Cardiff (Nash-Williams rev Jarrett 1969) were all doubtless supplied with both men and matériel by sea. All lie on tidal rivers (the Conwy, Seiont, Dyfi, Neath, and Taff respectively), and there were extensive *vici* at Caernarvon and Carmarthen. The Hen Waliau (Old Walls) at Caernarvon, lying 140 m west of the fort at the edge of the slope to the river, seem to be the remains of some kind of military stores depot, reminiscent of South Shields. No harbour installations have been found at any of these forts, but there would appear to be scope for limited exploration at several of them.

Caerleon, as headquarters of the II Legion, lies on the Usk estuary and, like Chester, would certainly have possessed extensive harbour installations. Fryer (1973, 267-8, fig 2B) describes the harbour installations excavated in 1963 (Boon 1964); the excavator estimated that the massive stone and timber wharf could have accommodated vessels of up to 5½ ft (1.67 m) draught at high tide.

Returning now to the east coast, there are two probable locations for military harbours, York and Brough-on-Humber. Fryer (1973, 267, fig 3A) discusses the evidence for wharves on the river Foss, which appears to have been wider in the Roman period than at present, and to have been tidal and navigable (RCHM 1962; Balmforth 1976). It is to be hoped that the excavation programme of the York Archaeological Trust will provide more evidence of Roman wharves in what was both a legionary fortress and a *colonia*, and must therefore have handled a considerable volume of waterborne trade.

The settlement at Brough-on-Humber (Wacher 1969) began in the 1st century as an auxiliary fort but was evacuated around AD 80; however, a military supply depot seems to have been maintained here, alongside a substantial civil settlement. The fort was reoccupied in the later 3rd century, perhaps as an outlier of the Saxon Shore system, to be abandoned in the last quarter of the 4th century. Brough is sited on a natural inlet of the Humber, and appears to have filled two military functions: like Brancaster on the Wash and Reculver on the Thames estuary, it guarded the approaches to an important waterway, but in periods of tranquillity it served as a port for the settled area between York and Lincoln. It was on Ermine Street and served as one terminal of a crossing matched by a small settlement at Old Winteringham (Stead 1976) on the opposite bank. Neither site has yielded evidence of harbour works: Wacher attributes this to the late Roman marine transgression, which swept away or submerged the existing structures.

The final group of military sites is the chain of forts on the south-eastern and eastern coasts. Some of these (Richborough, Lympne, Dover) appear to have been connected with the *Classis Britannica*: the recent excavations at Dover (Philp 1977) have established conclusively that there was a major Fleet establishment here in the 2nd and early 3rd centuries, and this may well have succeeded an earlier Fleet headquarters at Richborough (Cunliffe 1968, 255-60; Cleere 1977). The role of Lympne at this period is still not known, but it is hoped that the current excavations (Cunliffe 1977) will throw more light on this point. It is relevant to mention here a possible *Classis Britannica* port on the estuary of the river Rother at Bodiam, most likely used for the shipment of iron from the Fleet-operated ironworks in the Battle and High Weald areas (Lemmon & Hill 1966; Cleere 1974).

Nothing remains of any harbour works at Richborough, because of the coastal erosion/silting sequence that has carried away a substantial part of the fortifications. The important harbour at Dover has been brilliantly reconstructed by Rigold (1969), and additional information is coming to light as a result of the work of the Kent Archaeological Rescue Unit. There is an excellent chance of learning a great deal about the harbour at Lympne from Professor Cunliffe's excavations, since this site appears not to have been scoured so devastatingly as Richborough. The Bodiam site has only been sampled: it could yield much valuable information about a small specialized naval installation if excavated comprehensively.

Of the specifically Saxon Shore forts, Brancaster might be expected to provide information from excavation: the work of the Norfolk Archaeological Unit (Edwards & Green 1977) has provided spectacular air-photographic results, which suggest that the harbour lay to the northeast of the fort, near Brancaster Staithe. Burgh Castle has been subject to landslip on its western side, but 19th century excavations revealed traces of what may be harbour works (Johnson 1976, 37). Bradwell, guarding the Blackwater estuary, has been severely slighted, but fragments of a Roman harbour have been traced as submerged masonry outlines in an adjacent marshland (Johnson 1976, 44). Reculver has lost half its surface area to the sea and any harbour works will have disappeared, although underwater searching might provide some evidence of masonry structures. Pevensey has been attacked similarly and is unlikely to yield much evidence, but the Portchester site has been protected by the Isle of Wight from the strong south-westerly currents that have so profoundly altered much of the Roman south-eastern coastline; however, here the remains of the early harbour probably lie just below the waters that wash the western defences, and so exploration would only be possible at exceptionally low tides.

To summarize, then, sizeable Roman harbours may be anticipated at the legionary fortresses (Caerleon, Chester, and York), at Wallsend (for the Wall garrison), at Maryport and Lancaster (for the north-western defensive system), and at Dover, all of these probably acting as trans-shipment and distribution points for dependent coastal and inland military establishments. It would be reasonable in these cases to expect to find installations adequate to deal with seagoing vessels of the Blackfriars type. Smaller port installations, for the use of individual garrisons, may be postulated at the Welsh coastal forts (although forts such as Caernarvon and Carmarthen may have supplied inland establishments such as Y Gaer, Tomen-y-Mur, etc). If the Saxon Shore forts were naval bases, they would have required wharfage to accommodate fighting ships and transports. If, however, they are to be seen essentially as stores depots, the harbour installations could have been more modest.

One caveat needs to be entered regarding the military settlements. The Roman army was traditionally self-sufficient and accustomed to live off the land, both on campaign and on garrison duty. The volume of materials that would have been brought into military establishments would not have been large: wine and oil, some pottery, glass, and metal, and certain foodstuffs for units stationed in regions unsuitable for agriculture. In addition, there may have been some movement of troops by sea, on leave or on special assignments: at least one tombstone records the death of a legionary by shipwreck (*RIB*.I.544). Substantial quays would not have been necessary for relatively small movements of this kind. Those forts from which naval vessels might be expected to operate—Dover, the Saxon Shore forts, Brough-on-Humber—would, however, have needed something more elaborate to accommodate the biremes, triremes, and liburnians of the Fleet, together with repair facilities, and so there is perhaps a greater likelihood of finding more substantial or extensive remains at these forts.

Archaeological evidence of harbours from military sites will for the most part come from land excavations; however, underwater exploration might yield information at certain of the Saxon Shore forts, such as Pevensey and Portchester.

Civil ports

Reverting to the hypothetical Severn-Humber demarcation, it will be seen that there are a number of ports that may be postulated from the road map—Lincoln, Caister-by-Yarmouth, Colchester/Fingringhoe, London, Rochester, Hastings, Chichester, Fishbourne, Bitterne, Hamworthy, Radipole, Exeter/Topsham, Sea Mills, Gloucester, and Caerwent. A number—indeed, most—of these probably have military origins from the conquest period: Lincoln and Gloucester were legionary fortresses, Colchester and London were pivotal points in the early years of the conquest, and there is evidence of 1st century military use of Rochester, Fishbourne, Hamworthy, Topsham, and Sea Mills to supply the advancing legions.

However, it is proposed to examine these centres in terms of settlement and trade rather than their short-lived strategic significance. London was the pre-eminent trading centre of Roman Britain, and recent work in the City (eg Tatton-Brown 1974) has provided evidence of massive waterfront developments on either side of the presumed location of London Bridge. The Department of Urban Archaeology of the Museum of London has concentrated much of its effort on the waterfront over the past three years, and the results from the Custom House site, New Fresh Wharf, Seal House, Baynard's Castle, and Trig Lane suggest that wharves stretched continuously for more than 1 km on the north bank of the Thames (Hobley 1976). The richness of the finds from the City confirms the evidence of the waterfront and the nodal location of London in the road system of the province: London was the entrepôt for goods from the Low Countries and the Rhineland, a short sea crossing away, as well as from Spain and the Mediterranean, and would have been an equally important shipping port for exported goods, such as metals, hides, etc.

London's mercantile pre-eminence is indisputable; however, there are other towns whose central position in areas of intensive settlement and accessibility by water give them a special significance in terms of waterborne trade. Gloucester must have played a role not dissimilar to London's in the Roman west country. Fryer (1973, 262-4, fig 1) discusses the available evidence: a considerable frontage of wharves has been located in a now-silted creek protected from the heavy tides of the Severn and its famous bore. These were built in both timber and stone, implying a degree of substance and stability in trade and markets. Lincoln's role in the north-east was probably comparable. There is less evidence of harbour installations—only a 6 m stretch of dressed stone on an earlier river alignment (Fryer 1973, 264; Wacher 1974,

125)—but the Witham would have been navigable to this point, whilst in addition to the road network that radiates from Lincoln there may well have been access by water southwards via the Car Dyke, using flat-bottomed craft of the type known from London and the Netherlands.

The other port sites mentioned were less significant from the point of view of trade. Sea Mills probably served the important Mendip metal-producing region (Todd 1976, 102-4), and would, of course, have been a convenient port for shipping out its products. Topsham was the port for Exeter and Radipole may have served Dorchester, although a submerged structure a little farther west in Lyme Bay may have been the post for this area (R Holman, pers comm). Bitterne was probably the port for Winchester, although it may well have had wider connections, since pigs of Mendip lead have been found there. It also became a military centre in the 4th century, when the harbour at Portchester seems to have silted up (Johnson 1976, 141-2). Fishbourne (Cunliffe 1971) may have served Chichester, although there are a number of inlets comparable to Fishbourne Creek nearer to Chichester where the harbour for the town may have been located. Rochester would have served the rich villas on the North Downs, taking part-cargos from ships making for London, and might also have been the port from which the Kentish ragstone so favoured by Roman builders was shipped out. Fingringhoe was a natural outlet for Colchester (which it certainly served during the military occupation of the immediate post-invasion years). Caister-by-Yarmouth is the obvious entry port for the rich farmlands of East Anglia.

To these sites should be added Dover, which must have possessed a substantial civil port in addition to the military installations, and Brough-on-Humber, which was in effect a civil settlement for much of its life and seems to have served as a shipping port for Derbyshire lead (Wacher 1969). The possibility of there having been a port at Hastings has often been discussed, and its location has been suggested as offshore in the Bulverhythe area. The non-urban nature of the settlement in this part of the Weald, which seems likely to have been an Imperial estate throughout the Roman period, coupled with the apparent orientation of the minor roads in the area towards the Rother estuary port of Bodiam, suggests that this is one putative port that may be disregarded.

The situation in the Bristol Channel is worthy of study. As suggested above, Gloucester was probably the main port for the region. Caerwent may have had some installations, but probably on a relatively minor scale. There remains the problem of how the iron from the Forest of Dean which, like the Weald, was probably an Imperial estate (Cleere, unpublished) was shipped out. A case can be made out for some form of port at Lydney, although the nature of the site there does not suggest that it was of commercial significance. A more likely candidate might be Woolaston (Hudson & Scott-Garrett 1938), where the extensive villa had two bath-houses and a 'light guide-line, for guiding Severn craft through the Guscar rocks to its shore' (Hart 1967, 25).

So far, none of the minor ports surveyed above has produced clear evidence of harbour installations, with the exception of Fishbourne. There is little chance of the fairly slight remains being recovered by land excavation, but it might be that underwater exploration around some of them—in Lyme and Weymouth Bays, for example—could produce interesting results.

In summary, it may be said that there was at least one major civil port in Roman Britain (London), trading widely with the Mediterranean, Gaul, and the Rhine provinces; there were probably two secondary mercantile centres (Gloucester and Lincoln), serving regions remote from London, and perhaps with a bias towards trade with the Mediterranean and Gaul and with the Low Countries and the Rhine provinces respectively. Beyond these three major ports, the remaining harbours were in all probability small, with localized markets in their immediate hinterland.

In assessing the scale of likely installations in the smaller harbours, some attention should be given to the type of trade that was being carried on—the materials likely to have been shipped through them and their volume. If it is assumed that imports, such as wine, oil, fine pottery, glass, querns, and other 'luxury' goods, would have been brought into the province through the major ports, these smaller harbours need only have been large enough to receive relatively small vessels, bearing imported goods and British products not available in the immediate region—certain foodstuffs, a little trade in timber and building materials, and metals as either semi- or fully-finished products. There would also have been some movement of local products out of these harbours. For the most part, however, *civitates* were self-sufficient, and trade would have been on a very small scale, necessitating infrequent visits by relatively small vessels: the analogy would seem to be with the trade pattern in the China Sea and South Pacific until comparatively recently—small vessels plying a coastwise or island-to-island trade.

This is an important factor to consider when attempting to evaluate the likelihood of more evidence being forthcoming from deliberate exploration. There is considerable evidence already for harbour works at London and Gloucester; at these centres and at Lincoln, further exploration in city centres will be subject to the rescue situations that arise and will require the resources of the permanent teams in existence in these three cities. Opportunities may exist for limited exploration on land and underwater at some of the smaller port sites identified in the paper, but it should be recognized that the chances of finding remains of the relatively slight structures that probably existed are not good.

Conclusion

The pattern of Roman settlement in Britain—broadly, military in the Highland Zone north of the Severn-Humber line and civil to the south in the Lowland Zone—determines the location of harbours. The military harbours were sited with strategic considerations in mind, the civil ports for reasons connected with trade and the location of home markets. The pattern of the Roman conquest is reflected in the road system in the civil zone, with London as the major nodal centre and subsidiary centres (Lincoln and Gloucester) at former legionaries fortresses, utilizing military road communications. Other civil ports developed to supply *civitas* capitals on major trade routes or those less accessible by road from the larger ports. In the late 3rd and 4th centuries, the Saxon Shore defensive system introduced a series of purely military harbours at key strategic locations, protecting major inland waterways (Wash, Blackwater, Thames, Wantsum, Southampton Water). Of the military harbours in the Highland Zone, most were probably simple, serving individual forts; however, those at the legionary fortresses (Caerleon, Chester, York) and at Dover were probably considerably larger.

Most of the Roman harbour works are traceable only by
land excavation, owing to silting of estuaries, embanking
of rivers, and coastal changes. In a few cases, largely on
the south and east coasts, underwater archaeology may
be able to assist in the location and exploration of
submerged harbour works.

References

Balmforth, D J, 1976   in *The Church Street sewer and an adjacent
building* (J B Whitwell), *The Archaeology of York,* 3/1, 25.

Boon, G C, 1964   in Roman Britain in 1963, *J Roman Stud,* **54,**
152-3.

Cleere, H F, 1974   The Roman iron industry of the Weald and its
connexions with the *Classis Britannica, Archaeol J,* **131,** 171-99.

——, 1977   The *Classis Britannica,* in *The Saxon shore* (ed D E
Johnston), CBA Res Rep **18,** 16-19.

Cunliffe, B W, 1968   *Fifth report on the excavation of the Roman
fort at Richborough, Kent,* Soc Antiquaries Res Rep **23.**

——, 1971   *Excavations at Fishbourne 1961-1969—Vol 1: The site:*
Soc Antiquaries Res Rep **26.**

——, 1977   The British evidence: Lympne—a preparatory comment, in *The Saxon shore* (ed D E Johnston), CBA Res Rep **18,** 29-30.

Edwards, D A, & Green, C J S, 1977   The British evidence: the
Saxon shore fort and settlement at Brancaster, Norfolk in *The
Saxon shore* (ed D E Johnston), CBA Res Rep **18,** 21-9.

Frere, S S, 1974   *Britannia,* 2 edn.

Fryer, J, 1973   The harbour installations of Roman Britain, in
Marine archaeology (ed D J Blackman), Colston Papers **23,** 261-73.

Hart, C E, 1967   *Archaeology in Dean.*

Hobley, B J, 1976   The archaeological heritage of the City of
London, *London J,* **2,** 67-84.

Hudson, F, & Scott-Garrett, C, 1938   *Archaeol Cambrensis,* **23,**
93-125.

Jarrett, M G, 1976   Maryport, Cumbria: a Roman fort and its
garrison, *Cumberland Westmorland Antiq Archaeol Soc Extra
Ser,* **22.**

Johnson, S, 1976   *The Roman forts of the Saxon shore.*

Lemmon, C H, & Hill, J D, 1966   The Romano-British site at
Bodiam, *Sussex Archaeol Collect,* **104,** 96-102.

Livens, R G, 1974   Litus Hibernicum, *Actes IXe Congrès International d'Etudes sur les Frontières Romaines,* 333-9.

Nash-Williams, V E, 1969   *The Roman frontier in Wales,* 2 ed
(revised M G Jarrett).

Philp, B J, 1977   The British evidence: Dover, in *The Saxon shore*
(ed D E Johnston), CBA Res Rep **18,** 20-1.

RCHM, 1962   *An inventory of the ancient monuments in the city
of York,* I, *Eburacum, Roman York,* Royal Commission on Historical
Monuments, England.

RIB   Collingwood, R G, & Wright, R P, *The Roman inscriptions
of Britain,* **I,** 1965.

Richmond, I A, 1953   *The Roman fort at South Shields.*

Rigold, S E, 1969   The Roman haven at Dover, *Archaeol J,* **126,**
78-100.

Spencer, C, 1975   in *Archaeological excavations 1974,* 50-1,
HMSO.

Stead, I M, 1976   *Excavations at Winterton Roman Villa and other
sites in North Lincolnshire,* DoE Archaeol Rep **9.**

Tatton-Brown, T W, 1974   Excavations at the Custom House site,
City of London 1973, *Trans London Middlesex Archaeol Soc,* **25,**
117-219.

Todd, M, 1976   The *vici* of western England, in *The Roman West
Country* (eds K Branigan & P J Fowler), 99-119.

Wacher, J S, 1969   *Excavations at Brough-on-Humber 1958-1961,*
Soc Antiquaries Res Rep **25.**

——, 1974   *The towns of Roman Britain.*

Williams, J, 1970   in *Archaeological excavations 1969,* HMSO, 20.

Britain and the Rhine provinces: epigraphic evidence for Roman trade

Mark Hassall

Non-trading contacts

The scope of this paper is limited to the epigraphic evidence for trade. It is, however, worth surveying briefly first the evidence for non-trading contacts between Britain and the Rhineland. Like Britain, the Rhineland, consisting from the time of Domitian of the twin provinces of Germania Inferior and Germania Superior, was a frontier zone—the nearest section of the imperial frontier to Britain—and it is hardly surprising that the military histories of the two areas should, from the beginning, be intimately connected. Of the four conquest legions of Britain, no less than three were drafted from the Rhine garrison—legions II from Strasbourg, XIV from Mainz, and XX from Neuss. The evidence for this is largely epigraphic and has been surveyed by Ritterling (1924/5) for each of the legions concerned. Auxiliary regiments were also raised in, or withdrawn from, the Rhine frontier for the invasion. These included eight cohorts of Batavians raised in Lower Germany (Hassall 1970), numbering some 4,000 men in all, if quingenary, as is usually assumed (or just possibly as many as 6,000-8,000 if milliary in size). Our information is fragmentary but we know that among other auxiliary units were the *ala Indiana* (*RIB.I.* 108; Stein 1932, 141; Alföldy 1968b, 19) raised twenty years earlier from among the Treviri, and an *ala* of Thracians which, despite the reservations of Alföldy (1968b, 36), had probably seen service in Lower Germany before crossing over to Britain (*RIB*.I. 109).

This close contact between the two areas, evident at the time of the initial invasion of Britain, was subsequently maintained. Legionary detachments were sent as reinforcements from the Rhineland to Britain or vice versa as need arose (Saxer 1967). Vexillations from all four British legions fought in Southern Germany under Domitian (*ILS*. 9200 cf 1025), while others, amounting to 3,000 men drawn from Upper Germany and Spain, came to strengthen the army of Britain under Hadrian (*ILS*. 2726). Under his successor, Antoninus Pius, detachments from both Germanies came to Britain to strengthen the three British legions c 155 AD (*RIB*. 1322) and again in the early 3rd century (*J Roman Stud*, **57** (1966), 205, no 16; Birley 1967). With one or other of these groups will have come the unfortunate Junius Dubitatus of legion VIII who dropped his shield in the Tyne (*CIL*. VII. 495). Some of these soldiers lost more than their shields. An inscription from Caerleon (*RIB*. I. 369) was set up as a memorial to a soldier, presumably in legion II Augusta, *defun(c)tus expeditione Germanica*. Sometimes complete legions were moved, as when legion VI came to Britain from Lower Germany early in Hadrian's reign, probably sailing directly from the Low Countries to Newcastle, where it dedicated twin altars to Neptune and Oceanus (*RIB*. I. 1319 and 1320). Similarly, legion IX which left Britain sometime after 107/8 (*RIB*. I. 665), initially for Nijmegen (Bogaers 1965, 15-18, 21-3; Nesselhauf & von Petrikovits 1967). Auxiliary regiments, or parts of them, will have taken part in these movements between the two theatres: for example, the *ala Vocontiorum*, part of the British garrison, which is attested in the Low Countries (*ILS*. 2536; Bogaers 1965, 20-1).

Quite apart from such sporadic contacts, a very large proportion of the auxiliary forces stationed in Britain, especially the infantry, were of Germanic origin (Bang 1906). The evidence for the immediate conquest period has been reviewed above. For the later 1st century we have the evidence of Tacitus, who specifically mentions four cohorts of Batavians and two of Tungrians who served under his father-in-law (*Agricola*, ch 36) and the newly enrolled *cohors Usiporum per Germanias conscripta*, which mutinied in AD 83 (*Agricola*, ch 28). These seven units, all 'German', are in fact the only auxiliary regiments mentioned by the historian apart from certain British levies. For the 2nd century the military diplomas (*CIL*. XVI) provide us with many more names, while 2nd and 3rd century inscriptions and the *Notitia Dignitatum* give us not only some further names but allow us to assign garrison sites to units. From these sources we know that, in addition to the solitary *ala Tungrorum* known to be in the province by 98 (*CIL*. XVI. 43) and later attested at Mumrills on the Antonine Wall (*RIB*. I. 2140), these were no less than sixteen cohorts or part-mounted cohorts, out of a total of perhaps about 40, which were raised in the two Germanies or Gallia Belgica.

In the 3rd century new units, *cunei* and *vexillationes* of cavalry and *numeri* of infantry, were raised. We know of three distinct *cunei* of Frisii serving in the area of Hadrian's Wall, each bearing an epithet derived from the forts where they were stationed. There were also vexillations of Germans at Old Penrith and of Suebi at Lanchester at least as early as the 230s. There was a *numerus Hnaudifridi* at Housesteads ('Notfrieds Irregulars') and in the south the *numerus Turnacensium* at Lympne and *numerus Abulcorum* at Pevensey (*ND Occ*, LVIII, 15, 20) and *milites Tungrecanorum* at Dover (*ibid* 14). In other words, with rare exceptions, such as the Cananefates, every ethnic group west of the lower Rhine provided troops for the army of Britain, some, like the Nervii and Batavi in thousands, while even groups like the Frisii and Suebi east of the Rhine contributed too.

These units were not only raised in the Germanies or Gallia Belgica, but also preserved, at any rate for a period, their ethnic character once they had been sent to Britain, though how far this was through new drafts from their countries of origin it would be hard to prove. This ethnic character is shown by the numerous distinctive names of German origin belonging to the men who served in them, as shown by the inscriptions they set up, or which, as gravestones, were set up to them. Even when a soldier bears the *tria nomina* of a Roman citizen, a German origin is sometimes specified, or the *cognomen* may be the latinized form of a 'German' name. Sometimes whole groups within a particular unit preserved, at any rate at first, a separate corporate identity, as the *cives Tuihanti* from Twenthe, a group within the *Cuneus Frisiorum* at Housesteads (*RIB*. I. 1593, 1594), or the Texandri and Suve(vae?) part of a detachment of *cohors II Nerviorum* at Carrawburgh (*RIB*. I. 1538) or the men all from the same village (*pagus*) mentioned on another, damaged, inscription of the same unit from Wallsend (*RIB*. I. 1303). *Cohors II Tungrorum* was recruited, on the other hand, from at least two *pagi*, the *pagus Vellaus* and *pagus Condrustis* (*RIB*. I. 2107, 2108, Birrens).

The names of the gods and goddesses, whether west German or east Celtic, worshipped by the Rhinelanders and their neighbours once in Britain tell the same story (for some of the Germanic deities see de Vries 1956 & 1957 indexes). There were male gods who might be identified with Roman equivalents like Mars Thincsus (*RIB* I. 1593) and Hercules Magusanus (*RIB*. I. 2140; Horn 1970). There were also goddesses who were worshipped singly such as Viradecthis (*RIB*. I. 2108), Garmangabis (*RIB*. I. 1074), Harimella (*RIB*. I. 2096); or in pairs like the Alaisiagae (*RIB*. I. 1594), variously named Baudihillia and Friagabis (*RIB*. I. 1576) or Beda and Fimilena (*RIB*. I. 1593); or in trios, like the Matres who were distinguished by epithets such as Alatervae (*RIB*. I. 2135), Germanae (*RIB*. I. 1989), or the double epithet *Ollotatoe sive transmarinae* (*RIB*. I. 1030), both of which terms occur singly (*RIB*. I. 574, 1031, 1032, 919). The continental centre of the worship of the Matres was the middle Rhineland (de Vries 1957, 289 with distribution map). Of the male gods only the enigmatic Hviteres were worshipped collectively (Haverfield 1918; Heichelheim 1961; Frere 1971, 367; Birley 1953, 26-37 pl II. 6). A dedication from Old Carlisle to the *T[erra] Batavorum* (*RIB*. I. 902), if the reading is correct (Davies 1977), though more Romanized in concept, is equally significant in the present context.

If there were many German auxiliaries serving in Britain, there were, as might be expected, far fewer legionaries, though we know of two brothers from Xanten (Colonia Ulpia Traiana) who served in legion II Augusta at Caerleon (*RIB*. I. 357) and one man from the same place who died at Chester, and had presumably served in legion XX VV (*RIB*. I. 506). These correspond to the few men from Britannia who served in the Rhine legions (*CIL*. XIII. 6679, from Lincoln in legion XXII Primigenia at Mainz, or the *classis Germanica* (BRGK 40, 1959, 200f no 216). But in contrast to the large total of auxiliaries from the two Germanies and Gallia Belgica serving in Britain, only one regular cohort raised in Britain served in Germany. This was *cohors II Brit[tonum]* (or possibly *Brit[annorum]*) *milliaria equitata Civium Romanorum*, a Flavian foundation which served for a short period in the Rhineland, where it has left tilestamps at Xanten and Vechten (*CIL*. XIII, 12424f; Alföldy 1968b, 49-50; Bogaers 1969, 34). There were, however, a dozen or so *numeri Brittonum* serving on the Upper German frontier. Their first appearance there is thought by Baatz (1973, 71) to be contemporary with the earliest period of occupation of the fortlet of Hesselbach on the Odenwald limes, that is, between AD 95 and 105 (cf Wild 1975, 147).

If an auxiliary soldier from Germany was sent to Britain, he would normally remain there until discharge, unless his unit as a whole was withdrawn from the province. Postings for officers were more flexible, whether for the long-service centurions who might, on an initial appointment or subsequent promotion, move from province to province, or for the short-term spells of service of equestrian and senatorial officers and officials. Both sorts of transfer will have been common between the Rhine frontier and the British frontier. Thus, to cite one example only, Titus Domitius Vindex, who made a dedication to Mars Halamard(us?) at Horn near Roermond in Limburg, on which he describes himself as centurion in legion XX VV (*CIL*. XIII. 8707), was in fact probably, as Bogaers suggests (1962/3, 40-84), a *beneficiarius consularis* in legion XXX VV, who set up

his altar on hearing of his promotion to a centurionate in Britain. At a higher level, of the procurators who served in Britain, Julius Classicianus had Rhenish connections and was either a tribesman of the Treviri or Helvetii (PIR[2] *sub nomine*); and in the 2nd century a number of governors of the provinces took up their appointments immediately after the governorship of Lower Germany, as, for example, A Platorius Nepos, the builder of Hadrian's Wall, and Lollius Urbicus, the builder of the Antonine Wall. (Alternatively the governorship of Moesia Superior was commonly held before proceeding to Britain: Birley 1957, 10; Fitz 1961, 196.)

To summarize, it has been shown that whatever else did or did not travel from the Rhineland to Britain, personnel certainly did. Sometimes the troops and officials would travel by road westward to Boulogne, but sometimes they may have made the crossing direct from the Low Countries. Yet if the movement of important officials and military personnel between the two areas was regular, that of civilians was negligible. We know of two visitors at Bath from the Moselle area (*RIB*. I. 140 and 163) and that is virtually all. There are two dedications made to east Celtic deities like Mars Lenus (Gose 1955) from Caerwent, where one is to be definitely explained by the town's proximity to the nearby legionary fortress at Caerleon (*RIB*. I. 310) and the other probably so (*RIB*. I. 309). The reading of a dedication to Mars Lenus at Chedworth (*RIB*. I. 126) is not as secure as one would wish but it may be that the two dedications found in this country made in *honorem domus divinae* (*RIB*. I. 89, Chichester, and *Britannia*, 7 (1976), 378-9, no 2) were made by people with a 'Rhenish connection' since the formula is commonly found in the Rhineland. Conversely, we know of two men from Chester who travelled to the Rhineland (*CIL*. XIII. 6221, Worms) and the Moselle (*BRGK*, 17 (1927) 6, no 20, Trier).

Trading contacts

If the epigraphic evidence for the movement of the army and officials to and from the Rhineland is very full, that for traders is more meagre. From Britain itself there is indeed very little evidence for traders of any kind: an inscription from Bowness-on-Solway (*RIB*. I. 2059) was set up by a man about to embark on a trading mission, but one in north-western waters rather than across the North Sea. More to the point is a sarcophagus from York (Table II, no 7) of a tribesman of the Central Gaulish Bituriges Cubi, a *sevir Augustalis* of the colony and, if the interpretation put forward by J C Mann (Birley 1966, 228) is correct, a *moritex*, a Celtic word apparently meaning 'shipper' (Table II, no 7 with note). Another *sevir Augustalis*—of both York and Lincoln—Marcus Aurelius Lunaris, is known from an altar from Bordeaux that he set up in AD 237 (Table II, no 8). He is usually thought of as being concerned in the Bordeaux wine trade, but it is possible that, since he operated from the east coast of Britain, he may have had dealings with the Rhineland too. Evidence of a different kind is provided by a wooden writing tablet from London which refers to the construction of a ship—a tantalizing glimpse into the business archives of a shipper based on the provincial capital (*J Roman Stud*, 31 (1931), 247, no 2c). Finally, in 1976 part of a dedication slab was found at York. It was set up in AD 221 by the trader L Viducius Placidus, a tribesman of the Veliocasses of the Rouen area of northern Gaul (Table II, no 9). The dedicator is to be identified with the *negotiator Britannicianus*, Placidus son of Viducus, *cives Veliocassinius*, attested on an inscription from the shrine of Nehalennia near Colijnsplaat in Holland (Table I, no 5 and Appendix).

Table I   Traders and shippers at Colijnsplaat and Domburg

Name	Business	Origin	Reference
1 L Secundius Similis	*negotiator allecarius*		Stuart & Bogaers 1971, no 5=*AE* 1973, 365
2 T Carinius Gratus	*negotiator allecarius*		Stuart & Bogaers 1971, no 5=*AE* 1973, 365
3 C Gatullinius Seggo	*negotiator allecarius*	*cives Trever*	Stuart & Bogaers 1971, no 22=*AE* 1973, 375
4 Arisenius Marius (lib)	*negotiator Britannicianus*		Bogaers 1971(b), 35
5 Placidus Viduci fil	*negotiator Britannicianus* =Table II, no 9+Appendix	*cives Veliocassinius*	Stuart & Bogaers 1971, no 45
6 M Secund (inius?) Silvanus	*negotiator cretarius Britannicianus*		Stuart & Bogaers 1971, no 11=*AE* 1973, 370
7	*negotiator cretarius Britannicianus*		Hondius Crone 1955, no 25=*ILS* 4751
8 · · · · M · · · ·	*?[negotiator] Gallicanus?**		Stuart & Bogaers 1971, no 20=*AE* 1973, 374
9 M Exgingius Agricola	*negotiator salarius*	*cives Trever CCAA*	Stuart & Bogaers 1971, no 1=*AE* 1973, 362
10 C Jul(ius) Florentinus	*negotiator salarius*	*Agripp(inensis)*	Stuart & Bogaers 1971, no 4=*AE* 1973, 364
11 C Jul(ius) Januarius	*negotiator salarius*	*Agripp(inensis)*	Bogaers 1971(b), 37
12 Q Cornelius Superstis	*negotiator salarius*		Stuart & Bogaers 1971, no 25=*AE* 1973, 378
13 Commodus Ufeni(?)tis filius	(*negotiator vinarius*)		Stuart & Bogaers 1971, no 44
14 Bosiconius	*actor navis Flori Severi*		Bogaers 1971(b), 39
15 Vegisonius Martinus	*nauta*	*cives Secuanus*	Stuart & Bogaers 1971, no 13=*AE* 1973, 372

*For *negotiatores Gallicani* cf *CIL*. X. 7612 and XI. 5068 (=*ILS*. 7524). Alternatively, Gallicanus may be the *cognomen* of the dedicant.

The clearest epigraphic evidence for trade between Britain and the Rhineland comes indeed not from Britain but from the continent, and in particular the site near Colijnsplaat and the sister site of Domburg some 25 km to the west, off the north coasts of Noord-Beveland and Walcheren respectively. For Roman times, however, to describe the location of the two sites in this way would be meaningless. Then the estuary of the Scheldt lay further north than at present and neither Walcheren nor Noord-Beveland existed (Bogaers 1967b, 6, 102, fig 4). For Viducius and his contemporaries the site at Domburg lay south of the estuary mouth, while that near Colijnsplaat was further inland and north of the estuary. Both were shrines to the goddess Nehalennia near what were presumably important harbours: these harbours served ships trading between the Rhineland (via the Waal) and Gallia Belgica (via the Scheldt) on the one hand, and the coastal regions of Gaul and the east coast ports of Britain on the other, as the Viducius inscriptions have so graphically shown. Before leaving the sheltered waters of the estuary, it was not uncommon for traders to seek the protection of the goddess, whose name Nehalennia, or, probably more correctly, Neihalennia (Bogaers & Gysseling 1972a) means 'guardian' or

'guiding' goddess, by vowing to erect an altar to her on their safe return. On many of these altars the goddess herself is represented in flowing garments, either sitting with a dog beside her and a basket of fruits on her lap or sometimes standing with one foot on the prow of a vessel. The shallow depression or hearth (*focus*) often carved on the top of Roman altars is usually replaced by an 'offering table' on which are set either fruits or loaves. Domburg, where coastal erosion exposed the remains of her temple in the 17th century, has produced some 27 dedications to Nehalennia and five altars to Jupiter and Neptune (Hondius-Crone 1955). The site near Colijnsplaat, very probably the ancient Ganuenta, or perhaps Ganuentum (Stuart & Bogaers 1971, no 27; Bogaers & Gysseling 1972b) was located by the chance discovery of two altars brought up by trawling nets in 1970. Within the next twelve month a further 122 altars were recovered in a planned campaign of trawling and diving, many now illegible, but all probably dedicated to Nehalennia (Bogaers 1971b; Stuart & Bogaers 1971). These dedications, more than 150 of them from the two sites, sometimes with the reason for their erection clearly stated by the formula *ob merces recte conservatas* or its variants, will mostly have been set up after successful

Table II   Other traders and shippers

Name	Business	Origin	Reference
1 L Solimarius Secundinus	*neg(otiator) Britannicianus*	*civis Trever*	Bordeaux: *CIL*. XIII. 639
2 C Aurelius C L Verus	*negotiator Britannicianus, moritex*		Cologne: *CIL*. XIII. 8164(a)
3 Asprius A[. . .	*reversus [e]x Britannia*		Bonn: *BRGK* **27** (1937), 99, no 167
4 Fufidius	*[negoti] ator [?vesti] arius ex [Provinci] a Brit[annia]*		Cassel: *CIL*. XIII. 7300
5	*negotiator vestia[rius ex Britannia?] superiore*		Marsal: Gallia Belgica: *CIL*. XIII. 4564
6 L Priminius Ingenuus	*negotiator vestiarius importator*		Xanten: *CIL*. XIII. 8568
7 M Verecundius Diogenes	*sevir Augustalis*, York *moritex**	*cives Biturix Cubus*	York: *RIB*. I. 678; *J Roman Stud*, **56** (1966), 228
8 M Aurelius Lunaris	*sevir Augustalis*, York and Lincoln AD 237		Bordeaux: *J Roman Stud*, **11** (1921), 101-7,= *AE* 1922, no 116
9 L Viducius Placidus	*negotiator* [. . .] AD 221= Table I, no 5 & Appendix	*domo [civitate] Veliocas[s]ium*	*Britannia*, **8** (1977), no 18

*For *moritex*, compare no 2. An alternative interpretation, however, is preferred by J E Bogaers, who suggests that the reading is *III III vir Aug Col Ebor itemq(ue) Mori(norum)*, rather than *idemq(ue) morit(ex)*. Tervanna (Therouanne in the Pas-de-Calais), chief town of the Morini, is called *Colon(ia) Morinorum* on an inscription from Nijmegen (*CIL*. XII. 8727). For a man who held the post of *sevir* in two colonies, compare no 8.

landfall had been made either at the end of a one-way passage by sea or, more commonly, after the completion of a round trip.

What do these journeys—between 150 and 300 of them—mean in terms of the total volume of trade? To estimate this we would have to know 1. for how long the ports associated with the sanctuaries at Domburg and near Colijnsplaat were used; 2. whether a trader would set up an altar on average once a trip, once a year, or once a lifetime; and 3. what proportion of the altars originally dedicated have been recovered. Unfortunately we know the answers to none of these questions. As regards the first question we have the evidence of the coin series from Domburg (Boersma 1967, 68-70). This suggests that there were two periods of activity at the site: AD 69-238 and AD 260-73. The latter is linked by Boersma with defence measures taken against sea raiders, the former with trading activity. It is unlikely, however, that altars were set up at Domburg throughout the whole of the first period and it is tempting to link the dedication of most of them specifically to AD 180-218 when the coin series peaks. What is true of Domburg should be broadly true of the site near Colijnsplaat since the style of the altars from both places is similar and one man, Marcus Secund(inius?) Silvanus, (Table I, nos 6 and 7) makes dedications at both. However, two inscriptions from Colijnsplaat have consular dates of 223 (Stuart & Bogaers 1971, no 46) and 227 (*ibid* no 32; Bogaers 1972a), while Placidus son of Viducus, who also makes a dedication there (Table I, no 5) is now attested at York on an inscription which carries the consular date 221 (Table II, no 9). These dates (all within the decade 220-30) could be explained by supposing that Colijns-plaat remained of importance somewhat longer than Domburg. Alternatively they may simply reflect a contemporary epigraphic fashion for recording consular dates.

On the second question, only one man is certainly known to have made two dedications, the trader Marcus Secund(inius?) Silvanus mentioned above, although, it should be noted, the two altars were set up at different shrines. A second possible case is that of Hilarus, a decurion of Nijmegen, the Municipium Batavorum, who made the dedication in 227 at the shrine near Colijns-plaat. A fragment of an altar from the same shrine was set up by a trader whose name ends in -arus, and who was also a decurion of the municipium, but the actual identity of the two men is uncertain and is regarded by Bogaers as unlikely (1972a). Whether or not identity is assumed, on present evidence it seems possible that individual traders normally set up not more than one altar at each of the Nehalennia shrines. That they set up altars on the completion of every round trip is completely out of the question and less expensive expressions of thanks to the goddess must have been offered instead. Though, therefore, it is impossible to quantify the volume of trade that passed through the two ports implied by the shrines, the evidence does at the very least show that both were flourishing, especially in the last quarter of the 2nd century and the first half of the 3rd century AD.

Bogaers discusses the origins of the dedicants at the two sites (1971b, 37-8, plus corrections to Stuart & Bogaers 1971, nos 27 and 32 in Bogaers & Gysseling 1972b, and Bogaers 1972a). Attested are men from the Rouen and Besançon areas, Nijmegen, Trier, and Cologne, and Cologne (or strictly speaking Deutz) is the only place apart from the two Dutch sites to have produced dedications to Nehalennia (*CIL*. XIII. 8498 and 8499).

These origins largely confirm that the East Scheldt estuary acted as the outlet for goods to and from the Rhineland.

Much of the trade carried on by *negotiatores* mentioned on other inscriptions from sites in the Rhineland proper (*CIL*. XIII, index 13) will have been of a very local nature, but the mere presence of a trader at the Nehalennia shrines implies that he was concerned with trade further afield—either by river (the Scheldt) inland, or by sea, even if this was only coasting trade with Gaul. But since any particular trader at the two Dutch sites (with one possible exception: Table I no 8 and note) may have been concerned in trade with Britain, I shall consider all those cases where the trades of the dedicators are specified in discussing the sort of goods that were carried between the two areas. My debt here, as ever, to Professor Bogaers is very great (Bogaers 1971b, 40ff).

1 *Negotiatores allecarii* (Table I, nos 1-3) Dealers in a type of fish. *Al(l)ec, al(l)ex,* or *ha(l)lec* (Pliny, *Natural Histories* XXXI, ch 44(95)) was used as a relish on several of the dishes described by Apicius, the Roman writer on cookery. *Allecarii* are attested definitely only at Colijnsplaat (but note *CIL*. XIII. 8513, tentatively restored by Bogaers as *neg(otiator) a[llecarius]*). It may have been produced in Holland and Bogaers (1971b, 40 and pl 53) illustrates the sherd of a *dolium* found at Aardenburg with the inscription ALIIC XI S(emis)—eleven and a half amphorae or quadrantals of allec (about 300 litres)—incised before firing below the rim. It could equally have been produced in Britain.

2 *Negotiatores Britanniciani* (Table I, nos 4 and 5) Presumably traders concerned with the transport of the various goods and commodities, known from archaeology, which travelled to and from Britain, including contents of the bottle stamped CCA found at Silchester (Boon 1974, 263). These bottles, even if the letters do not stand for *colonia Claudia Agrippinensis* (Cologne), were probably made in the Rhineland (cf *CIL*. XIII. 10025, 112ff). *Negotiatores Britanniciani* are also known from inscriptions found at Bordeaux and Cologne (Table II, nos 1 and 2, cf no 3). The man from Bordeaux was, significantly, a Treveran, while the Cologne trader is interestingly described also as a *moritex*.

3 [?*Negotiatores*?] *Gallicani* (Table I, no 8 and note) The text of the single relevant inscription is damaged. If the word *negotiator* is correctly restored, the sole trader so described will have been engaged in general trading with Gaul.

4 *Negotiatores cretarii Britanniciani* (Table I, nos 6 and 7) The word *cretarius* is derived from *creta* = chalk or pipe clay (Oxford Latin Dictionary) and *negotiatores cretarii* or *artis cretariae* are usually explained as traders in fine pottery or pottery figurines. Inscriptions mentioning them, though lacking the epithet *Britannicianus*, are found in the Rhineland and eastern Gaul and southern Germany —at Wiesbaden, Mainz, Metz, Lorch, Sumelocenna and Cologne (*CIL*. XIII, index 13) as well as Bonn and Trier (*BRGK* **27** (1937), 104, no 188; *ibid* **40** (1950), 124, no 3). They will have traded in east Gaulish sigillata and Rhenish wares, including the famous motto beakers as well as clay figurines, both of which were exported from the Rhineland to Britain (Toynbee 1964, 420-2). Among the figurines found in this country (which include many pieces from the Allier region of Central Gaul) is one which has, interestingly, been identified as Nehalennia

(Jenkins 1952), although the identification has not been universally accepted. Other figurines made and stamped by Servandus of Cologne have also been found in Britain (*EE*. IX, no 1356, *J Roman Stud*, **59** (1969), 244, no 61, and *Britannia*, **5** (1974), 464, no 15).

5   *Negotiatores salarii* (Table I, nos 9-11) Four inscriptions from Colijnsplaat were set up by traders in salt, three of whom were domiciled at Cologne. Bogaers (1971b, 41) suggests that this may be significant: he points out that the trade was an Imperial monopoly and that concessions to deal in salt may have been made to men living at Cologne, the provincial capital of Germania Inferior, where they could be kept under close supervision. We know that in the Flavian period the production of government salt was carried out along the coast of Gallia Belgica: two inscriptions from Rimini (*CIL*. XI. 390 and 391) were set up by the *salinatores civitatis Menapiorum* and *Morinorum* respectively to C Lepidius L F Proculus, a centurion who had seen service in several legions including VI Victrix, then based at Neuss, from where he may have been sent to supervise the extraction. But Bogaers also raises the possibility that the salt was produced in Britain, and there is widespread and growing evidence for salt working in Roman times along the south and especially the east coasts of England as well as at inland sites (de Brisay & Evans 1975).

6   *Negotiatores vinarii* (Table I, no 13) Bogaers (1971b, 42) identifies one dedicant at Colijnsplaat as a wine merchant on the basis of the reliefs on the altar dedicated by him to Nehalennia: on its side are vine scrolls and beneath the inscription is the representation of a barge laden with barrels. A *negotiator vinarius* is attested at Bonn (*CIL*. XIII. 8105) and the evidence for the production of wine in the Moselle and Rhineland in the Roman period is extensive (eg Wightman 1970, 189-92), so that Commodus, who set up the altar at Colijnsplaat, was probably an exporter of wine from these two centres. Finds of barrels in Britain, Germany, and Belgium, when analysed, have turned out to be of silver fir and larch. The former is native to the Alpine and Pyrenean foothills while the latter is found only in the Alps, so although the wine contained in the barrels was not necessarily produced in precisely these regions, the barrels must have been and the presumption is that the vineyards cannot have been too distant. The evidence of the barrels, then, is that some wine was being imported to the Rhineland (see Bogaers 1974b, 42; Boon 1974, 263-6, and 1975, 52-67; Wightman 1970, 191, with discussion and further references on this complex question).

To summarize, the inscriptions from the two Nehalennia shrines show that pottery, and perhaps wine, were being exported to Britain, and salt and fish sauce were possibly imported from Britain in return. To these imports should be added woollen clothes (Wild 1967, 648-9). The men listed in Table II (nos 4, 5, and 6) could all have been importers of clothes from Britain such as the famous *birrus Britannicus*, known from Diocletian's Price Edict (XIX, 48), though in two cases crucial pieces of the inscriptions are restored and in the third there is no absolute proof that clothes were being imported from Britain, although this is quite likely. Some traders may have been exporters of some commodities, such as pottery, and importers of others, such as clothes (cf Messius Fortunatus *negotiator artis cretariae*, neg(oti-

ator) paenul(larius)—a dealer in pottery and cloaks (*CIL*. XIII. 6366) but located at Sumelocenna in Raetia and therefore perhaps unlikely to have been concerned with trade with Britain). Corn may also have been exported to the Rhineland, as it certainly was in the 4th century (Frere 1971, 390, 402, note 32), but we have no means of knowing whether the *negotiatores frumentarii* known from Aquae (Aachen: *CIL*. XIII. 7836) and Nijmegen (*CIL*. XIII. 8725) dealt with grain that was imported or grown locally.

Finally, something should be said about the evidence of epigraphy for the organization of trade. Here we may think of *corpora*, associations whether guilds (*collegia*), whose members had a common interest, or business partnerships (*societates*). Organizations of both types could have existed for both the traders (*negotiatores*) and the shippers (*navicularii*, *nautae*).

We know that at Wiesbaden the *negotiatores civitatis Mattiacorum* were banded together into a guild (either *collegium* or *corpus*) which had its own *schola* or clubhouse (*CIL*. XIII. 7587). Similar guilds, either general or for a particular trade or craft, almost certainly existed in all the major Rhineland towns, as well as towns like London and the *coloniae* of Colchester, York, and Lincoln. *Negotiatores* from other towns who had or shared *stationes* (offices), like those in the Piazza delle Corporazioni at Ostia (Meiggs 1973, 283-8; Calza 1915) away from home, may have banded together to form a *collegium peregrinorum*. Such *collegia* were not, as has been thought, groups of non-Roman citizens living in a city that had Roman rights, since they are attested after the *constitutio Antoniniana* of AD 212 when all free-born men in the Empire received citizenship, and members of some *collegia* are known who possessed the *tria nomina* of Roman citizens (Bogaers 1960/1, 306, note 232). *Collegia peregrinorum* existed at Silchester (*RIB*. I. 69, 70, 71; Boon 1974, 58) and in Holland at Voorburg-Arentsburg (Bogaers *op cit*). The individual *negotiatores Britanniciani*, *cretarii Britanniciani*, etc, may have formed themselves into guilds in view of their common interests, just as it can be assumed that the lessees of the fishing rights (*conductores piscatus*) among the Frisii did (cf *CIL*. XIII. 8830 = ILS. 1461: a joint dedication made by the lessees to the goddess Hludana). The shippers based at the different ports probably belonged to *collegia* too. One such is indicated at Fectio (Vechten) by an inscription which was set up by the *cives Tungri et nautae qui Fectione consistunt* (*CIL*. XIII. 8815 = *ILS*. 4757).

There is a temptation to think of the *negotiatores Britanniciani* or *negotiatores cretarii Britanniciani* as not merely guilds but actual companies on the model of those that are presumed to have operated the *stationes* around the Piazza delle Corporazioni at Ostia. Even at Ostia, however, the *stationes* may simply have been offices shared by groups of traders or shippers from the same town, rather than run by actual companies as such. Business associations are more likely to have been very small affairs. L Secundius Similis and T Carinius Gratus (Table I, nos 1 and 2), who made a joint dedication at the shrine near Colijnsplaat, will certainly have been business partners. Sometimes a business will have been a family affair, and there is evidence for three generations of the same family all making dedications at Colijnsplaat (Bogaers 1971b, 32). Some business associations may have consisted of both active and sleeping partners who put up capital. Shipping, too, will have been in the hands of both individual *nautae* and small *societates*. The smaller shipowners or the active members of partnerships will have operated their own vessels (Table I, no 15), but the larger owners will have employed *actores navium*, agents to represent them on board ship. One such was Bosiconius, the *actor navis* of Florius Severus (Table I, no 14). *Actores* may also have been employed by the larger companies of *negotiatores*, although it is likely that most of the dedications at the two Dutch sites were made by merchants or shippers rather than their agents.

In conclusion, though the epigraphic evidence for trade between Britain and the Rhineland is sparse, the finds from the two Nehalennia shrines give us indications both of the extent of the trade in the late 2nd and early 3rd century and how that trade was organized. Evidence from Britain is at present largely lacking, but the recent discoveries of the Viducius dedication at York, and of altars built into the riverside wall of Roman London (*Britannia*, 7 (1976), 378, nos 1 and 2) show that this is due only to the accident of survival, and we are fortunate indeed that the two Dutch sites have given us so much.

Appendix: The inscription of Lucius Viducius Placidus from York (Table II, no 9; cf I, no 5)

```
1  NEPTVNO]▼ ET GENIO LOCI
   ET▲NVMINIB ▼ AV]GG ▲ L ▲ VIDVCIVS
   VIDVCI▼F▼PLA]CIDVS DOMO
   CIVITATE ▼]VELIOCAS[S]IVM
5  PROV▲LVGD▲N]EGOTIATOR
   BRITANN ▼ AR]CVM ET IANVAM
   PRO SE ET SVIS DE]D[IT] GRATO ET
   [SELEVCO▼ COS]
```

Neptuno] et Genio Loci | [et Numinib(us) Au]g(ustorum) | L(ucius) Viducius | [Viduci f(ilius) Plac]idus domo| [civitate] Veliocas[s]ium | [prov(inciae) Lugd(unensis) n]egotiator | [Britann(icanus) ar]cum et ianuam | [pro se et suis de]d[it Grato et | [Seleuco co(n)s(ulibus)]

'To Neptune and the Genius of the place and the Deities of the Emperors, Lucius Viducius Placidus, the son of Viducius, from the canton of the Veliocasses in the province of Lugdunensis, trader with Britain, presented the arch and gate in the consulship of Seleucus and Gratus (AD 221)'

The left-hand part of the dedication is missing (Fig 43a) and, with the exception of the beginnings of lines 2 and 3, the restoration offered here (Fig 43b) differs from that of Roger Tomlin who first published the inscription in *Britannia*, 7 (1977), no 18). Notes on the present restoration follow:

1.1 Neptuno. Compare the dedication to Neptune from Domburg (Hondius-Crone 1935, no 36). Tomlin suggests *I(ovi) O(ptimo) M(aximo) D(olicheno)*, which is too short if the restoration given here of 1.3 is correct.

1.3 Placidus's filiation in this form occurs on his dedication to Nehalennia from the shrine near Colijnsplaat, and should be the only possible one since Viducus, the father, lacked a praenomen, or rather the full *tria nomina* of a Roman citizen.

1.5 For the inclusion of the province, compare the description of M Aurelius Lunaris (Table II, no 8) as *sevir col Ebor et Lind Prov Brit Inf*.

1.6 Restored on the basis of Placidus's dedication to Nehalennia, where he is described as *negotiator Britannicianus*. A possible objection to the use of the epithet *Britannicianus* here would be that, since the dedication was found at York, there would be no need to describe Placidus as a trader *with* Britain. However, if the *negotiatores Britanniciani* formed a guild of traders, as has been suggested above (p 45), this objection loses its force. The reading IANVAM seems epigraphically preferable to FANVM (*Britannia, loc cit*).

1.7 The phrase *pro se* or *pro se et suis* occurs on seven of the altars erected to Nehalennia at her shrine near Colijnsplaat (Bogaers 1971b, 39).

The main point of interest lies in the fact that Placidus is the first *negotiator* of all those who made dedications to Nehalennia to be attested on this side of the Channel. It is also interesting to note that on his Nehalennia dedications he has a single name, Placidus, appropriate to a man who lacked Roman citizenship (*peregrinus*)*, whereas on the York stone he has the *tria nomina*, Lucius Viducius Placidus, of a Roman citizen. It is quite possible that Placidus gained citizenship as a result of the *constitutio Antoniniana* in 212, when all free-born *peregrini* living within the Empire were granted this status. He will have formed a *nomen* from the single peregrine name of his father. If this is correct, his Nehalennia dedication should date to before the year 212, and it could be argued that this is also true of other dedications to the goddess where the dedicator has a single peregrine name, but the language is otherwise full and formal. On the basis of this argument six of the dedications from the shrine near Colijnsplaat should have been erected before this date.

Acknowledgement

I am most grateful to Professor J E Bogaers, on whose published writings this paper leans so heavily, for making extensive corrections to a draft version of it. He does not, of course, necessarily subscribe to all ideas expressed, nor can he be held responsible for errors that it may contain.

Abbreviations used in the text

AE   *Année Epigraphique* in *Revue Archéologique* (Paris)

Ber ROB *Berichten van de Rijksdienst voor het Oudheidkundig Bodemonderzoek*

BRGK *Bericht der Römisch-Germanischen Kommission* (Frankfurt/Main-Berlin)

CIL   *Corpus Inscriptionum Latinarum* (Berlin 1863)

EE   *Ephemeris Epigraphica*

ILS   *Inscriptiones Latinae Selectae* ed H Dessau (Berlin 1892-1916)

PIR² *Prosopographia Imperii Romani* 2nd edition, Berlin 1933—in progress

RE   Paulys *Realencyclopädie der classischen Altertumswissenschaft*, Neue Bearbeitung Wissowa-Kroll-Mittelhaus (Stuttgart 1894)

---

*It is very unlikely that Placidus simply omitted his *praenomen* and *nomen*, since he included both filiation and tribal origin.

Fig 43   Inscription of L Viducius Placidus from York: a surviving inscription; b suggested reconstruction

RIB   *The Roman Inscriptions of Britain*, R G Collingwood and R P Wright (Vol I, Oxford 1965)

ND Occ *Notitia Dignitatum* (in partibus Occidentis) ed O Seeck 1876 (reissue Frankfurt 1962)

References

Alföldy, G, 1968a   Epigraphisches aus dem Rheinland III, *Epigraphische Studien*, **5**, 1-98.
——, 1968b   Die Hilfstruppen der römischen Provinz Germania Inferior, *ibid*, **6**.
Apicius   The Roman cookery book, edition of text of the *Artis Magiricae Libri X* and translation by Barbara Flower & Elizabeth Rosenbaum.
Baatz, D, 1973   Kastell Hesselbach und andere Forschungen am Odenwaldlimes, *Limesforschung*, **12**.
Bang, M, 1906   *Die Germanen im römischen Dienst bis zum Regierungsantritt Constantinus I.*
Birley, E B, 1953   The Roman fort at Netherby, *Trans Cumberland Westmorland Antiq Archaeol Soc*, **53**, 6-39 & pl II, fig 6.
——, 1957   Beförderungen und Versetzungen im römischen Heere, *Carnuntum Jahrbuch*, **3**, 3-20.
——, 1966   Review of R G Collingwood and R P Wright, *The Roman Inscriptions of Britain 1: Inscriptions on Stone* in *J Roman Stud*, **56**, 226-31.
——, 1967   Troops from the two Germanies in Roman Britain, *Epigraphische Studien*, **4**, 103-7.
Boersma, J S, 1967   The Roman coins from the Province of Zeeland, *Ber ROB*, **17**, 65-97.
Bogaers, J E, 1960/1   Civitas en stad van de Bataven en Canninefaten, *ibid*, **10-11**, 263-317.
——, 1962/3   Ruraemundensia, *Archaeologische Werkgemeenschap Limburg, uitgave bij gelegenheid van het eerste lustrum 1963-8*, 13-43. Originally published in *Ber ROB*, **12/13**, 57-86 with addenda.
——, 1965   De bezettingstroepen van de Nijmeegse legioensvesting in de 2de eeuw na Chr, *Numaga*, **12**, 10-37.
——, 1967a   Die Besatzungstruppen des Legionslagers von Nijmegen im 2. Jahrhundert nach Christus, *Studien zu den Militärgrenzen Roms, Vorträge des 6. Internationalen Limeskongresses in Süddeutschland, Bonner Jahrbücher*, Beiheft **19**, 54-76.
——, 1967b   Einige opmerkingen over het Nederlandse gedeelte van de limes van Germania Inferior (Germania Secunda, *Ber ROB*, **17**, 99-114.
——, 1969   *Cohortes Breucorum, ibid*, **19**, 27-50.
——, 1971a   Some notes in connection with the Dutch section of the *limes* of Germania Inferior (Germania Secunda), *Roman Frontier Studies 1967, The proceedings of the Seventh International Congress held at Tel Aviv* (eds M Gichon & S Applebaum).
——, 1971b   Nehalennia en de epigrafische gegevens, *Deae Nehalenniae Gids bij de tentoonstelling Nehalennia de Zeeuwse godin, Zeeland in de Romeinse tijd, Romeinse monumenten uit de Oosterschelde*, 33-43.
——, 1972a   Van Nijmegen naar Nehal(a)en(n)ia, *Numaga*, **19**, 7-11.
——, 1972b   Civitates und Civitas-Hauptorte in der nördlichen Germania inferior, *Bonner Jahrbücher*, **172**, 310-33.
Bogaers, J E & Gysseling, M, 1972a   Over de naam van de godin Nehalennia, *Naamkunde*, **4**, 3-4, 221-30. Originally published in *Oudheidkundige Mededelingen uit het Rijksmuseum van Oudheden te Leiden*, **52**, 79-85.
——, 1972b   Nehalennia, Gimio en Ganuenta, *Naamkunde*, **4**, 3-4, 231-40. Originally published in *Oudheidkundige Mededelingen uit het Rijksmuseum van Oudheden te Leiden*, **52**, 86-92.
Boon, G C, 1974   *Silchester: the Roman town of Calleva.*
——, 1975   Segontium fifty years on: 1, *Archaeol Cambrensis*, **124**, 52-7.
Brisay, K W de, & Evans, K A, 1975   *Salt, the study of an ancient industry.*
Calza, G, 1915   Il Piazzale delle Corporazioni e la funzione commerciale di Ostia, *Bulletino della Commissione Archaeologica Communale di Roma*, **42**, 178-206.
Davies, R W, 1977   Ateco of old Carlisle, *Britannia*, **8**, 271-4.
Diocletian   Price Edict, ed S Lauffer.
Fitz, J, 1961   Legati Legionum Pannoniae Superioris, *Acta Antiqua*, **9**, 159-207.
Frere, S S, 1971   *Britannia, a history of Roman Britain*, rev edn.
Gose, E, 1955   *Der Tempelbezirk des Lenus Mars in Trier*, Trierer Grabungen und Forschungen 2.

Hassall, M W C, 1970   Batavians and the Roman conquest of Britain, *Britannia*, **1**, 131-6.
Haverfield, F, 1918   Early Northumbrian Christianity and the altars of the Di Veteres, *Archaeol Aeliana*, ser 3, **15**, 22-43.
Heichelheim, F M, 1961   Vitiris, *RE*, **9** A 1.
Hondius-Crone, A, 1955   *The temple of Nehalennia at Domburg.*
Horn, H G, 1970   Eine Weihung für Hercules Magusanus aus Bonn. Mit einem Nachtrag von Henning Wrede, *Bonner Jahrbücher*, **170**, 233-51.
Jenkins, F, 1952   Nameless or Nehalennia, *Archaeol Cantiana*, **70**, 192-200.
Meiggs, R, 1973   *Roman Ostia*, 2 edn.
Nesselhauf, H, & Petrikovits, H von, 1967   Ein Weihaltar für Apollo aus Aachen-Burtscheid, *Bonner Jahrbücher*, **167**, 268-79.
Ritterling, E, 1924/5   Legio, *RE* **12**.
Saxer, R, 1967   Untersuchungen zu den Vexillationen des römischen Kaiserheeres von Augustus bis Diokletian, *Epigraphische Studien*, **1**.
Stein, E, 1932   *Römische Beamte und Truppenkörper im römischen Deutschland unter dem Prinzipat* (reissued 1965).
Stuart, P, & Bogaers, J E, 1971   Catalogus van de monumenten, *Deae Nehalenniae, Gids bij de tentoonstelling Nehalennia de Zeeuwse godin, Zeeland in de Romeinse tijd, Romeinse monumente uit de Oosterschelde*, 33-43.
Tacitus, Agricola   *Cornelii Taciti De Vita Agricolae*, eds R M Ogilvie and Sir Ian Richmond.
Toynbee, J M C, 1964   *Art in Britain under the Romans.*
Vries, J de, 1956   *Altgermanische Religionsgeschichte*, Vol **1**.
——, 1957   *Altgermanische Religionsgeschichte*, Vol **2**.
Wightman, E M, 1970   *Roman Trier and the Treveri.*
Wild, J P, 1967   The Gynaeceum at Venta and its contents, *Latomus*, **26**, 648-76.
——, 1975   Review of Baatz 1973, *Antiq J*, **54**, 1, 146-7.

The Rhine and the problem of Gaulish wine in Roman Britain

D P S Peacock

Introduction: Commercial routes between Britain and the Mediterranean

It is well known that quantities of Mediterranean amphorae are found in Iron Age, Roman, and post-Roman Britain. The presence of these vessels at once poses the question of the routes by which they were shipped, although this problem has seldom been considered because until recently we were largely ignorant of essential distributional data. Of course, Bonnard (1913) long ago discussed the various ways of traversing Gaul, based upon an assessment of the ancient authors and of geographical factors. There is little point in reiterating the burden of his thesis, but it is perhaps worth recalling that as an alternative to the Narbonne-Bordeaux route goods could be shipped up the Rhône, without doubt the principal commercial axis of Gaul. This vital step northwards to Britain could be used in a number of ways. Firstly, goods could be offloaded at Lyon and then transported overland to Roanne, whence the Loire would provide access to Britain via Nantes. Alternatively the journey could be continued via the Saône and the Plateau de Langres to the Seine. The Rhine could be reached by branching from the Saône along the Doubs and thence overland via the Col de Montbéliard, or by continuing northwards across country from the Saône to the Moselle. There are, of course, a number of minor variants but these are the main arteries, and to them should be added the long sea route via the Straits of Gibraltar and the Atlantic seaboard of Iberia and France. While the perils of voyages on Atlantic waters may have deterred extensive use of this route, it may have been important in certain periods. For example, the Bi, Bii, and Biv amphorae of the post-Roman period (Thomas 1959) are well known in the Mediterranean and in western Britain but apparently not in the interior of Iberia or France despite increasing availability of data.

It appears that amphorae and other Mediterranean goods could have arrived in Britain in a number of ways, begging the question not only of the route, but also of the economic or political factors determining the choice. Clearly, cost must have been an important parameter, though one that is difficult to assess. However, Duncan Jones (1974, 366) has considered the implications of Diocletian's Price Edict and, using this and other information, calculates that inland waterways cost 4.9 times as much as sea transport while haulage overland cost between 28 and 56 times as much. Of course, the evidence is slight, which raises the question of the validity of calculation. However the sea, river, and road ratio for early 18th century England is strikingly similar (1:4.7 and 1:22.6) and it seems that the few Roman transportation costs available to us are about the norm for developing countries at the present day (Clark & Haswell 1967, 184-8). These diachronous comparisons are, of course, open to debate but they do suggest that the economics of transportation by similar means may be governed by common factors in many early state societies, which gives grounds for accepting Duncan Jones's assessment. If the figures are reliable enough to be used as a basis for argument, they might permit economic assessment of the above routes and hence help

evaluate, within broad limits, their desirability as a means of transporting Mediterranean goods to Britain.

In each case the distance by sea, river, and land can be measured, the riverine distance multiplied by the lower rate of 4.7 and the land by 22.6. Addition of the distance by sea to the weighted river and land values will give a theoretical figure which should be proportional to the basic cost of that route. Some values are indicated in Table III, where it will be observed that the long sea voyage is cheapest, though in practice the risk factor may have militated against this.

Of the remaining routes, it can be seen that the Narbonne—Bordeaux link is cheapest and thus this is the one we might expect to be used in supplying the British market. The Rhine is theoretically twice as expensive and hence, if we find it used to supply the British market, this must be regarded as an economic anomaly worthy of explanation.

Dressel 30: The Gaulish wine amphora

The flat-based amphora, Dressel form 30 or Callender form 10 (Callender, 1965; cf Pelichet 1946), is one of our less well known amphorae, although it is much commoner in Britain than is generally appreciated and can claim to be one of the more important types. On the continent the form has a long life ranging from the 1st century BC at Cacerés to the 3rd century AD at Kastel Niederbieber (Beltrán 1970, 527). In Britain it is found in post-Boudiccan contexts at Colchester (Hull 1963, 188), but the main *floruit* appears to be in the latter part of the 2nd century. At Gloucester, for example, Dressel 30 comprises 15% of all amphorae from levels of that date (Hurst 1972). Persistence into the 3rd century is difficult to prove conclusively on British evidence alone, but it might be implied by finds such as a handle from Clausentum found in 3rd century levels (Cotton & Gathercole 1958, fig 26, 9).

The origin of this type has long been problematical. Callender (1965, 19) asserted that it was South Gaulish in origin, though he gave neither reason nor authority for this statement. Fortunately, firm evidence has now come to light which suggests that this attribution is correct, for Tchernia and Villa (1977) have recently published a kiln found at Velaux, near Marseilles, and amongst the products are Dressel form 30.

Gagnière (1969) reported an amphora kiln at Fours (Sauveterre), north of Avignon, but unfortunately he did

Table III — Theoretical comparison of costs to Britain

Route	Theoretical cost index
Sea from Narbonne via Gibraltar	4,440
Narbonne—Bordeaux via Aude & Garonne	5,779
Rhône—Loire via Lyon & Roanne	8,354
Rhône—Seine via Plateau de Langres	9,321
Rhône—Rhine via Saône and Doubs	11,038
Rhône—Rhine via Saône and Moselle	12,082

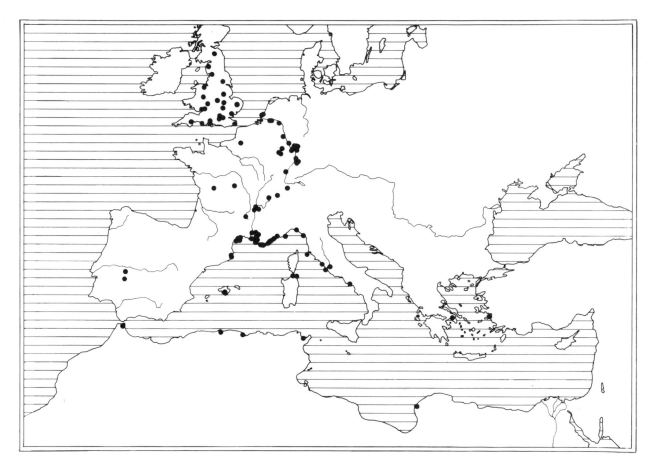

Fig 44   Distribution map of Dressel 30 amphorae

not record the types produced, although Panella (1973) has since investigated the matter and has ascertained the presence of this form. Another kiln which could have been used in the production of Dressel 30 was found twenty years ago at St Cyr-sur-Mer, not far from Toulon, but Benoit's (1956) note contains insufficient data to be certain of its relevance.

Thus, the evidence, such as it is, points to a concentration of activity around the mouth of the Rhône. The emerging pattern suggests a scatter of small concerns rather than a large factory, a view supported by petrological study, for there is appreciable textural variation within the samples examined. However the main components comprise quartz, mica, limestone, and rocks of metamorphic origin, all appropriate to the sediments at the mouth of the Rhône or around the Gulf of Lyons.

Southern France appears to be the main production region but the form was certainly made elsewhere. Vessels in a distinctive brown fabric are known from Portugal but their distribution appears to be restricted to south-western Iberia, and an analogous form was made in Algeria (Panella 1972). The latter might be confused with southern Gaulish vessels on typology alone, but museum study suggests that the Mauretanian products are rare and they are unlikely to bias the distribution map significantly. In addition, Dressel 30 appears to have been made in small quantities in north-eastern Spain (Pascual 1977).

Unfortunately *tituli picti* are very rare, making it difficult to assess contents. However, Panella (1973) has reviewed the evidence thoroughly, drawing on both ancient and modern works, and she convincingly argues that wine was the most important commodity.

The distribution of this form is very striking indeed (Fig 44). There is a marked concentration along the Mediterranean coast of France, up the Rhône, and particularly along the Rhine. There is no suggestion that the western seaways were employed in a significant way. As I have suggested, a distribution such as this demands an explanation, for it does not immediately make economic sense. One possibility that must be seriously considered is that it is a sampling phenomenon resulting from meticulous work in Germany and Holland. This can be dismissed on two counts. Firstly, other types of amphorae such as North African cylindricals (Peacock 1977) or Dressel 1 (Peacock 1971) show totally different distributions. Thus amphorae have been recorded from the blank parts of the Dressel 30 map and, had the latter been present in quantity, it is reasonable to suppose that at least some would have been recorded.

Further evidence comes from the study of bas-reliefs, conveniently available in Espérandieu's (1907-38) corpus. The much illustrated piece from Cabrière d'Aygues, Provence (Espérandieu, no 6699), shows amphorae on a quay and they are clearly the local product, Dressel form 30. In the north, the form is readily recognizable on the Neumagen reliefs, where the shape of rim and handles are clearly discernible (no 5216). Espérandieu also illustrates flat-bottomed amphorae from Cologne (no 8555) and in a sketch of reliefs from Arlon, Belgium (no 4072, unfortunately lost), all of which could be representations of Dressel 30. These northern finds come from the area of greatest concentration on the distribution map and they provide an independent link between the Rhineland and the mouth of the Rhône.

If these arguments are accepted, the distribution must be regarded as valid archaeological evidence and the problem remains: why ship goods to Britain via the Rhine, rather than the cheaper Narbonne—Bordeaux route? The answer must surely be that Britain was not the primary commercial objective, but the goods were destined in the first instance for the Rhineland, where a high civilian and, above all, military population provided a lucrative market. Perhaps Britain merely received the surplus when this market had been satisfied. However, it is more probable that the answer lies in the mechanism of transportation: in the complex organization and synchronization required to load and unload goods for different sectors of the journey. Having established a system to meet prolific Rhenish requirements it would be logical to use the North Sea link to carry goods to Britain.

Provence and the Aquitaine

This assessment of the distribution of Dressel 30 suggests that wine from southern Gaul was being transported to Britain via the Rhineland from the 1st to the 2nd and probably into the 3rd century AD, which raises the question of the relationship of the trade to that of the Aquitaine, long supposed to be a principal supplier of Britain in the 3rd century. Richmond (1946; 1955, 172; and in Callender 1965, 56) long ago observed that in Britain amphorae are much more common in the first two centuries AD than in the later Roman period. He suggested that in the earlier centuries Spain had been an important supplier of wine but the trade was disrupted by the Albinus-Severus episode, culminating in the battle of Lyons in AD 197. Britain and Spain had supported the losing side and, in reprisal, the Spanish estates were confiscated and their produce directed from Britain to the other parts of the Roman world. Thereafter Britain received its wine from Aquitaine, shipped in barrels rather than amphorae. This hypothesis found support in the well known Lunaris inscription linking Bordeaux and York, and in the barrels from Silchester, which are made of silver fir, a native of the Pyrenees (cf Richmond 1955, 172). In addition there is historical evidence suggesting that wine growing was established in the Aquitaine at an early date (Columella, iii, 2, 19).

Unfortunately, this attractive hypothesis is no longer so secure because certain key points are now invalid. Firstly, the basic *raison d'être* of the argument must be questioned because it is now generally agreed that the common globular amphora (Dressel form 20) held olive oil rather than wine (see, eg, Panella 1973 for a review of the evidence). Secondly, the silver fir employed in the barrel making has little significance. It is a montane species, but its natural habitat is wide and our knowledge of palaeobotany is so rudimentary that we have no means of ascertaining how far it had spread from its area of origin by Roman times. Thirdly, Boon (1975) has recently published an assessment of barrels in Britain and Europe, from which it is clear that the main concentration is along the river Rhine, and thus it is from there that the British examples probably derive, rather than Atlantic France. There is in fact very little evidence from Atlantic regions. An inscription from Nantes refers to *cuparii*, but there is no secure evidence that viticulture was established in *pays Nantais* before the 7th century at the earliest (Dion 1959, 155). Furthermore, Nantes is today near an area noted for salt production and there are indications of Roman as well as Iron Age working in

Loire Atlantique (Tessier 1975). Thus the manufacture of barrels need not automatically imply wine growing.

On the other hand the evidence from Bordeaux is more difficult to contest for, in addition to the Lunaris altar, an inscription set up by L Solimarius Secundus, engaged in trade with Britain, stresses the connection, which is further reinforced by British finds of pottery decorated *à l'éponge*, presumably made somewhere between the Loire and the Gironde (Fulford 1977, 45). However, the evidence is circumstantial and provides no proof that wine was involved or of importance in the trade. It is thus very difficult to make comparisons with the southern Gaulish commerce so clearly attested by the Dressel 30 amphorae transported in profusion along the Rhine.

Acknowledgements

One of the advantages of conference proceedings is that the published papers have often benefited from both formal and informal discussion with interested colleagues. In this case, the criticism of Mr G C Boon, Mr J P Gillam, and Professor K Hopkins helped to shape the present paper from a hastily prepared lecture. My views are unaltered, but they are, I hope, better argued for the comments I received.

References

Beltrán-Lloris, M, 1970   *Las ánforas romanas en Espana.*
Benoit, F, 1956   XIIe Circonscription Historique, Saint-Cyr-sur-Mer, *Gallia*, **14**, 231.
Bonnard, L, 1913   *La navigation interieure de la Gaul à l'époque gallo-romaine.*
Boon, G C, 1975   Segontium fifty years on: 1, *Archaeol Cambrensis*, **124**, 52-7.
Callender, M H, 1965   *Roman amphorae.*
Clark, C, & Haswell, M, 1967   *The economics of subsistence agriculture.*
Cotton, M A, & Gathercole, P, 1958   *Excavations at Clausentum 1951-54.*
Dion, R, 1959   *Histoire de la vigne et du vin en France.*
Duncan Jones, R, 1974   *The economy of the Roman Empire.*
Espérandieu, E, 1907-38   *Bas reliefs de la Gaule romaine.*
Fulford, M G, 1977   Pottery and Britain's foreign trade in the later Roman period, in *Pottery and early commerce* (ed D P S Peacock), 35-84.
Gagnière, S, 1969   Sauveterre, *Gallia*, **27**, 409.
Hull, M R, 1963   *The Roman potters' kilns of Colchester,* Soc Antiquaries Res Rep **21**.
Hurst, H, 1972   Excavations at Gloucester, 1968-1971: first interim report, *Antiq J*, **52**, 24-69.
Panella, C, 1972   Annotazioni in margine alle stratigrafie delle terme ostiensi de Nuotatore, *Coll Ecole Franç Rome*, **10**, 69-106.
——, 1973   Appunti su un gruppo di anfore della prima, media e tarda età imperiale, in *Ostia 3* (Studi Miscellanei. **21**).
Pascual Guasch, R, 1977   Las ánforas de la Layetanie, *Coll Ecole Franç Rome*, **32**.
Peacock, D P S, 1971   Roman amphorae in pre-Roman Britain, in *The Iron Age and its hillforts* (eds M Jesson & D Hill), 161-88.
——, 1977   Roman amphorae: typology, fabric and origin, *Coll Ecole Franç Rome*, **32**.
Pelichet, E, 1946   A propos des amphores romaines trouvées à Nyon, *Zeit schweiz Arch und Kunstgeschichte*, **8**, 189-209.
Richmond, I A, 1946   Part of the stem of a Roman monumental *candelabrum* of stone from York, *Antiq J*, **26**, 1-10.
——, 1955   *Roman Britain.*
Tchernia, A, & Villa, J P, 1977   Note sur le matériel recueillé dans la fouille d'un atelier d'amphores à Velaux (B du R), *Coll Ecole Franç Rome*, **32**.
Tessier, M, 1975   The protohistoric salt making sites of the pays de Retz, France, in *Salt, the study of an ancient industry* (eds K W de Brisay & K A Evans), 52-6.
Thomas, A C, 1959   Imported pottery in Dark Age western Britain, *Medieval Archaeol*, **3**, 89-111.

Roman trade between Britain and the Rhine provinces: the evidence of pottery to *c* AD 250

Kevin Greene

An assumption which often underlies discussions of Britain's trade in the Roman period is that Germany was in some way a 'natural' trading partner for this island. It seems to have developed from two sources: one, perfectly valid, is ancient; the other is modern, and its validity is therefore open to question.

The modern source results from the way in which Roman studies have developed in Europe. The early appearance of the *Limeskommission* of the German Archaeological Institute led through its very choice of subject to fieldwork, excavation, and the subjection of the materials recovered thereby to an increasingly technical form of study. The strongly text-oriented and art-historical procedures which have dominated most French and Italian work until recent years were relatively unimportant to the study of ill-documented, complex military frontier works. The importance of pottery to the latter was soon recognized by scholars like Knorr, Ritterling, and Loeschke, and their work still commands as much respect as its subject retains its relevance. The importance of this style of archaeology to Britain was obvious, with its lack of comprehensive documentation, its military emphasis, and complex frontier works. One has only to look at Curle's Newstead report of 1911 to see the influence of early German pottery reports, with their accurate measured drawings and attention to the whole range of vessels, not simply those which attracted attention through aesthetic appeal. It is often forgotten that some of Sir Mortimer Wheeler's first research was into the importance of Roman pottery from Germany for British archaeology.

Two wars have done nothing to reduce the growth of pottery studies in Germany and Britain. Gose and Gillam produced typological syntheses of the Rhineland and northern Britain in 1950 and 1957, while the *Limesforschungen* of the German Archaeological Institute and the Research Reports of the Society of Antiquaries of London, as well as numerous national and local periodicals, have devoted more space than ever before to systematic studies of Roman pottery from major sites. Meanwhile, important pottery studies have, of course, come from France, but their style has continued to owe much more to art-historical methodology. The result is that for detailed publications of pottery processed by comparable means on the Continent, the British archaeologist is inevitably led to Germany, the Netherlands, and Switzerland. The probability of finding connections between Britain and the Rhine provinces is therefore exceedingly high.

The other reason for seeking close links between Britain and the Rhineland is a real one, based upon the study of the many historically attested military connections between the two areas. The evidence is too familiar to require reiteration here, and is included in Hassall's paper (*above*, 41-8). Geographical factors would seem to provide further reasons for seeking close trading links: the mouth of the Rhine and the Thames Estuary seem ideally situated, whilst the Wash, Humber, and Tyne also provide inlets to important military and civil areas. The purpose of this paper is to illustrate that, despite academic and historical connections, Gaul, not Germany, was the 'natural trading partner' of Britain as far as pottery was concerned.

The way in which Britain received imports of pottery obviously depended on the way in which Roman pottery industries developed in the north-western provinces. Before any Roman merchants or troops appeared, Greek cities had been trading with Gaul, and even beyond to Britain and southern Germany. As well as amphorae containing wine, some tableware was traded as early as the 7th century BC. The trade network was presumably inherited in 121 BC by the Roman acquisition of the province of Gallia Narbonensis. The campaigns of Caesar in the 50s BC would have required elaborate arrangements for quartermastering, which must have stimulated the development of the economic life of the rest of Gaul, which then grew peacefully up to the next great military venture, the conquest of Germany. An enormous amount of industrial change must have taken place in the early stages of romanization; in the pottery industry, the tastes of Roman garrisons and coloniae would have exerted an important influence on the already highly competent native Gaulish potters. Foreign industries appeared: 'arretine' samian was produced in large quantities at the La Muette factory site in Lyon under Augustus together with other fine wares of Italian derivation (Lasfargues 1972).

This was the situation when Augustus's armies advanced to the Rhine, and briefly beyond it. The pottery found on sites like Oberaden and Haltern on the Lippe reflects this kind of background (Loeschke 1909; Albrecht 1939 and 1942). Most coarse pottery was made on the spot in an Italian tradition already tinged by Gaulish influence; Italianate fine wares and samian came mostly from Lyon, and in addition drinking vessels and tableware came from the so-called 'Gallo-Belgic' industries (Vegas 1975, 48-9). The pattern remained similar throughout the 1st century AD, although other centres in Gaul had superseded Lyon in the production of samian, and Gallo-Belgic wares gradually declined in importance. Coarse ware production remained in the (ultimately) Italian tradition, and only changed very slowly. When local fine-ware and samian industries developed to a more important position in the 2nd century, their output tended to be counterparts of Gaulish items, which did not travel far from their production sites. Rhineland pottery did not become at all important for Britain until the late 2nd century, and even then it seems that the establishment of factories in Britain itself might be preferable to seaborne trade. Most of the apparent links between Britain and the Rhine provinces are more indicative of similar sources of supply than direct contacts.

Two categories of pottery will be used in this paper to support these general observations: colour-coated ware and samian. A preliminary statement on terminology must be made.

'Colour-coated ware'

Unfortunately, the terminology applied to this category of pottery varies greatly, and is impossible to clarify satisfactorily. The term 'colour-coating' has the advantage of having no technical meaning: it is purely descriptive. It refers to a slip—almost always different in colour from the clay body—on the surface of a pot. Not all slips are colour-coatings, however; the consensus of usage is that the latter must be fine and reflective, whether actually glossy or matt. Other terms enter the field at the higher end of the scale of quality: 'gloss', 'varnish', and even 'glaze' are encountered in descriptions of the finest surfaces. 'Metallic' is often found as a qualification of some of these; again, it has no technical meaning, but describes a certain quality of lustre. In this paper, 'colour-coating' will be used to cover all of these terms except for a simple low-fired slip. A white surface coating on a mortarium or flagon of a different body colour would by this definition be a slip, even though it may be as good as the lower end of the spectrum of quality found on 'colour-coated ware'. This inconsistency can only be defended by the fact that the categories rarely overlap in any way that causes difficulty.

'Samian ware'

A similar inconsistency is encountered in the case of 'samian ware'. Continental terminology employs 'terra sigillata' to cover the whole range from Arretine to Argonne ware. 'Samian' will be used in this paper because of its normal use in Britain, and because the term was employed by Pliny (*Historia Naturalis*, XXXV, 12, (46), 160) irrespective of precise geographical origin, in the same way that 'china' is today. The principal problem lies not in terminology but in the fact that the characteristic surface of samian is simply a well-fired fine red colour-coating. This has been pointed out frequently but needs restating here. Thus the surface of what is called 'Rhenish ware' by archaeologists in Britain is the exact counterpart of the coating of samian. The only difference is that it has been fired in a reducing atmosphere to produce a black colouring. Although in practice the ranges of vessels made in the two fabrics were different, they do overlap, with the curious result that some reduced moulded or appliqué vessels made by samian potters are called 'black samian' whilst identical plain or barbotine-decorated vessels are simply 'colour-coated' (Simpson 1957; 1973).

Trade in colour-coated wares
The 1st century AD

The colour-coated vessels of the 1st century AD are almost all drinking cups or beakers, which played an important role as an auxiliary tableware used alongside samian or metal vessels. Their diverse forms can mostly be traced back to simpler Republican vessels.[2] The use of colour-coating increased during the reign of Augustus, and reached a peak in the Claudian-Neronian period (Greene 1972). Elaborate fine-ware vessels with colour-coated and even lead-glazed surfaces formed part of the ceramic complex which appeared in Lyon under Augustus; they were produced there by branches of established Italian workshops. The supply of garrisons on the Rhine and much of the Upper Danube was already substantially based on these Lyon factories under Augustus (Vegas 1969-70, 124, Abb 24). By the reign of Claudius, the Lyon colour-coated vessels had diverged away from their Italian counterparts (Fig 45, no 3) as much as La Graufesenque samian had from Arretine. Vessels from the industry which made the distinctive 'raspberry cups' between *c* AD 40 and 70 were traded as far as York to the north and the Magdalensberg, Austria, to the east, and sold heavily between these extremes (Fig 45, nos 1, 5). I have discussed elsewhere

the overall pattern of mid 1st century trade in colour-coated wares, but it may be repeated that comparable vessels reached Britain from seven continental sources (Greene 1973). A table of discoveries published in 1973 (*ibid*, 28) is substantially unchanged, except that recent finds have sent the products of the Lower Rhineland (Fig 45, no 2) to the bottom of the table, whilst the discovery of further Spanish cups (Fig 45, no 4) means that there are now more than six times as many vessels from southern Spain as from the Rhineland in Britain. If the assumption that the occurrence of vessels from sources other than Lyon may reflect the movement of other cargoes rather than a specific trade in pottery trade is correct, the implications for overall trade with the Rhineland may be important.

c AD 70-140

The period after the reign of Nero until the end of that of Hadrian is marked by a comparative lack of variety in colour-coated wares, and the simplicity of forms probably allowed much wider production which would minimize trade. The simple cornice-rimmed beaker (Gillam 1957, type 72: here, Fig 45, no 7), with its low girth and almost uniformly drab surface colouring and wide range of fabric colours (from white to brown and all shades in between), makes the identification of production centres and their distribution patterns difficult. However, a distinctive industry based in central Gaul was the source of a number of readily recognizable vessels (Fig 46, nos 1-3) and subjective observations of fabrics suggest that some cornice-rimmed beakers may have come from the same area. Without a programme of scientific analysis, it is not possible to show whether other cornice-rimmed beakers were or were not imported from the Rhineland, but their great variety and comparative simplicity argues for the making of many in Britain itself.

The Antonine industries

Although their scale was modest, the Vespasianic-Hadrianic industries maintained the tradition of production of a range of drinking vessels in colour-coated ware. The Antonine period saw a flowering of this tradition, which was to last down to the end of Roman pottery production in the north-western provinces. Its origins can be seen in the unbroken Mediterranean fine-ware tradition of the 1st and early 2nd centuries. Elaborate foliage in barbotine found in northern Italy (Fig 45, no 3) together with lively animals in Spain (Fig 45, no 4) probably lie behind the *'raetische Firnisware'* of southern Germany and Switzerland, an area which had always maintained connections across the Alps. The application of this decorative tradition to the cornice-rimmed beaker form—which had likewise maintained an unbroken development in the western Mediterranean area (Fig 45, no 6)—produced the familiar 'hunt-cup' (Fig 45, no 8).[3]

Although this newly popular colour-coated ware industry was important in the Rhineland, there is no evidence for export to Britain. It is indeed inherently unlikely, as similar industries were established in the Nene Valley and at Colchester by the 150s AD.[4] The white fabric of many of the vessels made in the Nene Valley makes them so similar to Köln products that trade in either direction would be difficult to detect, but at the same time unlikely.

The Colchester industry is directly linked with the Rhineland because of its association with sigillata

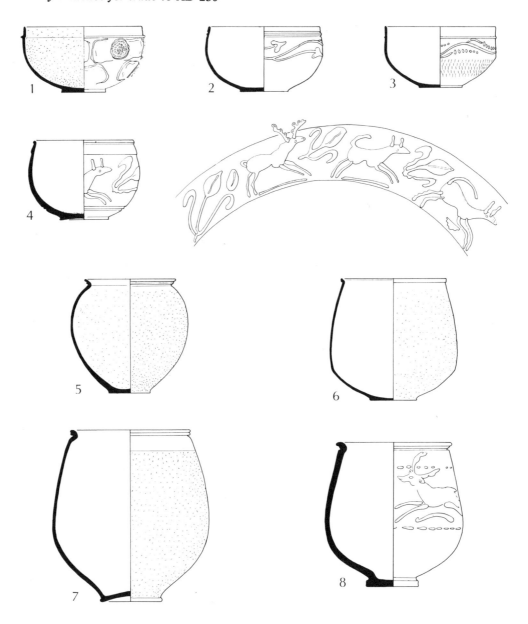

1   Lyons ware cup, type 5.2 (Greene 1972). Fine greenish-cream fabric, green-brown colour-coating. Plastic leaves and berries, fine sand internally. From Ubbergen, Nijmegen, Neths; Rijksmuseum van Oudheden, Leiden, e 1931/3. 820.

2   Lower Rhine cup, cf Greene 1972, fig 6, no 8.1. Fine white fabric; orange and brown colour-coating. Barbotine scroll and leaves. Utrecht, Neths; Centraal Museum I 396. 3132.

3   North Italian cup. Fine grey fabric; shiny black colour-coating. Turin region; Museo di Antichità, Turin.

4   Spanish (Baetican) cup. Mayet 1975, pl XLIX, no 412, and p 88. Fabric not described, but the ware is normally fine and buff with a reddish or golden-brown colour coating. Barbotine decoration. Probably from Belo, Portugal.

5   Lyons ware beaker, type 20.3 (Greene 1972). Fine cream fabric; orange-brown colour coating. Fine sand internally, coarser externally. Hunerberg, Nijmegen, Neths; Rijksmuseum van Oudheden, Leiden, e 1905/11.93.

6   South/Central Italian beaker. Fine brown fabric with grey outer skin. Dark brown-black metallic colour-coating. Sand externally. Cosa, Italy; American Academy in Rome.

7   Cornice-rimmed beaker. Gillam 1957, fig 9, type 72.

8   'Hunt-cup'. Gillam 1957, fig 10, type 85.

Fig 45   Miscellaneous colour-coated vessels (scale 1:3)

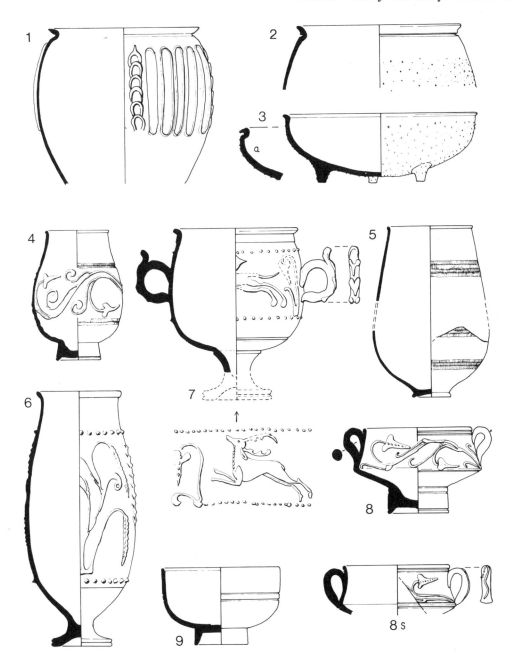

Flavian-Hadrianic types

1 'Hairpin beaker'. Fine buff fabric; chocolate brown colour-coating with orange patches; metallic sheen. Barbotine decoration. Vichy, Allier, France; Groupe de Fouilles de Terre-Franche, Vichy et Environs.

2 Cornice-rimmed beaker. Buff micaceous fabric; dark-brown metallic colour-coating. Clay particles externally. Gloucester; excavations by H Hurst, 77/69 XXXIII (98).

3 Tripod bowl. Buff micaceous fabric; chestnut brown colour coating. Clay particles externally. Kingsholm, Gloucester; excavations by H Hurst, 44/72 I (18). Because this vessel may be pre-Flavian, a more typical Flavian-Hadrianic rim form is added (3a), from Verulamiam; Frere 1972, 283, fig 107, no 234.

Antonine types

4 Beaker. Orange fabric; dark grey-brown colour coating. Barbotine decoration. Verulamium; Frere 1972, 343, fig 131, no 1056.

5 Beaker. Red fabric; black metallic colour-coating. Bands of fine rouletting. Gloucester; excavations by H Hurst. 74/68 I (22). The form is also found in *Moselkeramik aus Niederbieber* 31 (Oelmann 1914).

6 Beaker. 'Pinkish drab clay with metallic glaze'. Barbotine decoration. Richborough, Kent; Bushe-Fox 1926, pl XXX, no 134.

7 Handled bowl. 'Reddish clay with a good black glaze'. Barbotine decoration. Richborough, Kent; Bushe-Fox 1932, pl XLII, no 365.

8 Handled cup. Orange fabric, buff near surface, containing mica; lustrous black colour-coating. Barbotine decoration. 'Probably from Britain'; National Museum of Wales, Cardiff. The Central Gaulish origin of the form is confirmed by 8S in standard samian fabric, from Harvey Lane Chapel, Leicester; Jewry Wall Museum.

9 Cup. Red fabric, lustrous black colour-coating. Colchester, Essex; British Museum (Dept of Prehistoric and Romano British Antiquities), 54-4-12, 14.

Note: there is not space in this paper to argue the attribution of the above vessels to Central Gaul. I have examined many sherds in France and Germany, upon which fabric judgements are based. Some of the arguments about forms have been discussed by Brewster (1972).

Fig 46   Colour-coated vessels from central Gaul (scale 1:3)

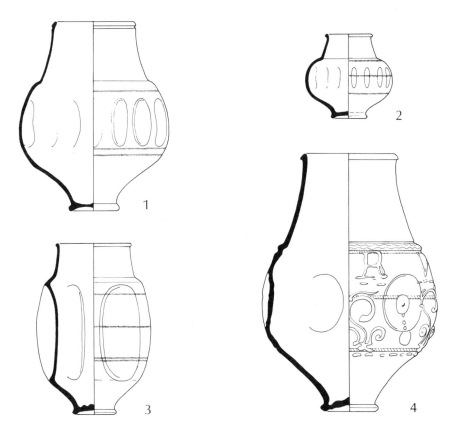

1 Indented beaker. Gillam 1957, fig 6, type 44, from Corbridge.
2 Indented beaker. Gillam 1957, fig 6, type 45, from Carrawburgh.
3 Indented beaker. Gillam 1957, fig 7, type 46, from Corbridge.
4 Indented 'motto-beaker' with white slip inscription (DA MERVM) and decoration. Verulamium; Frere 1972, 347, fig 133, no 1114.

Mosel vessels have a distinctive fine hard red and grey layered fabric (the layers can vary enormously in relation to each other), with a few small yellow-white inclusions. This is easily distinguished from the more varied Central Gaulish fabrics, which are rarely layered with grey and often contain mica.

Fig 47   Moselkeramik ('Rhenish ware') (scale 1:3)

production by potters who had come from the Sinzig/ Trier complex (Hull 1963, 85-9). In the Nene Valley, a good case has been made for the exotic connections of Indixivixus, a minor and idiosyncratic potter whose vessels can be related to East Gaulish sigillata forms (Dannell 1973). In the light of this potter and those working at Colchester, it may be assumed that this whole Antonine industrial assemblage was introduced from eastern Gaul or the Rhineland. The implication would seem to be that it was easier to establish foreign work-shops than to trade directly.

'Rhenish ware'

However, one distinctive ware was imported into Britain in the Antonine period—'rhenish ware'. Its range of finely thrown vessels, often with elaborate slip or barbotine decoration, and superb high-fired fabric and glossy or 'metallic' lustrous black coating was superior to any of the products of the British kiln sites (Fig 47). A distribution from Aquileia to northern England emphas-izes its commercial success. Its apparent indication of trade with the Rhine provinces is due entirely to its false name in British usage. The ware comes not from the Rhineland, but from sites from Trier through to central Gaul. In Germany it is called *Moselkeramik*—accurate-ly, since most (if not all) of it was made in Trier, and its central Gaulish equivalent (Fig 46, nos 4-8) is not found there.[5]

Fortunately, the products of central Gaul can be clearly distinguished from those of Trier by both their fabrics and forms. The remaining percentage not clearly assignable to either source presumably reflects the ability of lesser centres between Trier and Lezoux to make similar wares on a smaller scale. What is important is that none of the 'rhenish ware', irrespective of precise source, need necessarily reflect trade with the Rhine-land: from Trier a route west to the Marne or a tributary of the Seine would be as feasible as direct shipment down the Mosel to the Rhine. The date at which imports of Mosel/Central Gaulish 'rhenish ware' ceased is uncer-tain, but is unlikely to have been after the middle of the 3rd century.[6] There is after this no evidence of importation of fine colour-coated wares into Britain on any scale.

Trade in samian ware

The conclusions reached in the study of colour-coated wares will next be compared with the more secure histories of the changing trade patterns of samian ware.[7] Pre-conquest 'Arretine' from sites in Britain probably came from both Lyon and Arrezzo. Only analyses can quantify this, as their products are virtually indis-tinguishable. The Lyon production disappeared by the end of the reign of Augustus, and then South Gaulish kiln sites such as La Graufesenque became prolific exporters in the reign of Tiberius, and gradually drove Italian samian out of its transalpine markets along the Danube, and then Italy itself. The vivid testimony of the packing case of South Gaulish bowls found at Pompeii shows that this process was complete before AD 79 (Atkinson 1914). The whole of Gaul, the Rhineland, and Britain were supplied from factories in southern Gaul with vast quantities of their well made and very serviceable vessels.[8] Whatever economic or political circumstances brought the wide trade in elaborate colour-coated drinking vessels to an abrupt end in *c* AD 70 also seems to have affected the samian manufacturers. The rapid simplification of forms and decoration towards the end of the century seems to indicate an urgent need to speed production.[9] The last South Gaulish samian which reached Britain between *c* AD 90 and 110 is thick and poorly made; decorated bowls were pulled out of their moulds still damp, so that what poor scenes existed were often largely obliterated.

Around the very end of the 1st century, an improvement in clay mixtures in central Gaul led to the production of a fabric as practical as any South Gaulish ware (Picon 1973, 96-102). Samian had been made in the Lezoux area as early as in southern Gaul, but was scarcely exported until this improved ware was developed (Boon 1967). With a very few rare exceptions, Central Gaulish ware had completely replaced South Gaulish samian in Britain by AD 120. The Rhineland was supplied rather differently. Potters migrated eastwards as suitable clay sources allowed and a number of East Gaulish factories soon dominated their large local markets. Their products diverged permanently away from their early artistic links with parent factories in southern and central Gaul.

However, Central Gaulish ware sold well in south Germany and along the Upper Danube. East Gaulish sigillata first appears in quantity in Britain in the second half of the 2nd century, principally in its eastern regions and in the northern military area. It seems from the decline in the number of Central Gaulish potters active in the late Antonine period that East Gaulish ware may only have been making up for a falling supply from that source, rather than competing successfully against a strong rival. Certainly, it did not increase significantly in the 3rd century after the cessation of imports from central Gaul. When barbarian raids damaged East Gaulish factories in the mid 3rd century, an industry appeared around Oxford making what is by any definition samian in both form and fabric (Young 1973). Much of Britain existed thenceforth without this ware, but its popularity in much of central and southern England may explain why later East Gaulish ware was scarcely imported at all.[10]

How much of the samian made at Rheinzabern on the Rhine near Speyer travelled to Britain by way of the Rhine itself may be questioned: as with 'rhenish' ware from Trier, land and river routes to the Meuse, Somme, or Seine may have been just as convenient for cross-Channel trade. But concentrations of finds on Britain's east coast would seem to support some direct shipping from the Rhine.[11]

Conclusions
Samian ware
The well documented history of the shifting patterns of this industry seems to show that sigillata from East Gaulish kiln sites entered Britain in small quantities partly by the default of the Central Gaulish factories, and that trade did not increase after this competition had disappeared. The attempt by East Gaulish potters to establish a samian workshop at Colchester (Hull 1963, 43ff) is a possible indication of difficulties in direct trade.[12] East Gaulish samian was equally unsuccessful in trade into Gaul or south to the Upper Danube area; there, local kiln sites and Central Gaulish ware supplied a large proportion of samian requirement. Even with the modest quantities of East Gaulish ware which reached Britain, there is no certainty that a direct trade along the Rhine was always used.

Colour-coated ware
The pattern of the Claudian-Neronian period is very similar to that of 2nd century samian; a centre in Gaul possessed an enormous market embracing Britain, Gaul, and the Upper Danube provinces, whilst in the Lower Rhineland very competent local versions of the same vessels were made, but were hardly exported outside their production area, either south by river, inland to Gaul, or across the Channel. In both cases, one may ask whether the local demand of the concentration of major civilian and military centres was such that there was little surplus for export. The industries of Gaul, beginning with those of Lyon under Augustus, had always reached a wide area of dispersed markets.

The Antonine colour-coated ware upsurge in Britain seems to have been based on industries which came from the Rhineland, possibly in recognition of the difficulties of (or lack of existing framework for) direct trade. Only some of the highest quality colour-coated ware came from anywhere near the Rhine—*Moselkeramik* from Trier—and that may not always have travelled by way of the Rhine. A proper understanding that much of this so-called 'rhenish ware' came from central Gaul is important in emphasizing the overwhelming significance of that area's industries.

Trade with the Rhine provinces may thus be stated to have been negligible as far as pottery was concerned, and the pattern could be extended to other wares such as mortaria and the 'Gallo-Belgic' range. Nor should we be surprised, for in Gaul, according to Strabo (IV, 1, 2)[13]:

> '. . . the courses of the rivers are so excellently disposed in relation to one another that goods can be conveyed through from either sea to the other; for the cargoes must be conveyed over the plains for only a short distance and that without difficulty while for most of the journey they travel by the rivers . . . One may think that the workings of Providence are confirmed, the land being arranged in no random fashion, but as though in consonance with a reasoned plan.'

Notes
[1] Space has not allowed a discussion of the mechanics of Roman trade. The distribution of pottery and other cargoes was undoubtedly not the result of planned buying and selling, or production for clearly defined markets. We are left with a small proportion of the tangible evidence for a complex web of the individual and often random threads of countless transactions. The picture of medieval trade presented by Fulford (below, pp 59-69) must be borne in mind: so too must the fact that all the imported colour-coated vessels found in Britain could be fitted into a remarkably small number of packing-cases. The many modernisms in my terminology cannot be avoided without a full discussion of *mercatores, negotiatores,* and others whose activities are now represented only by potsherds.

[2] The development can be seen very well in general terms in Moevs's study of fine wares from Cosa, Italy (1973). Their dating and descriptive framework must be treated with extreme caution, however.

[3] Further examples of North Italian barbotine work—Schindler-Kaudelka 1975, Taf 20; Spanish barbotine work—Mayet 1975, pls XLIX-LVI. Both continued at least to the end of the 1st century AD, and overlap with the Flavian 'Raetian' colour-coated ware, which proceeded into the 2nd century to provide a link with hunt-cups. Several vessels are illustrated by Drexel from Faimingen (1911, 80-4).

[4] Evidence comes from the Verulamium fire deposit of c AD 155 (Frere 1972, 321, fig 122, nos 780-96).

[5] A good selection of finds from the Trier production site is included in Oelmann's Niederbieber report (1914, 36, Abb 12-13).

[6] Only two sherds have been found in the extensive excavations at Portchester Castle, which began its occupation around AD 280 (Fulford 1975, 279 and 315, fig 173, no 27).

[7] Full details can be found in Oswald & Pryce (1920), although the section on the earliest South Gaulish ware and its relation to Arretine is now outdated by finds in Lyon (Lasfargues 1972). More briefly, see Hartley (1969) or Johns (1971).

[8] South Gaulish ware also entered Spain, North Africa, and even sites in the eastern Mediterranean, before *terra sigillata Hispanica* and African red-slipped ware developed fully.

[9] The disappearance of cup forms such as Dragendorff 24/25, Ritterling 8 and 9 to leave only Drag 27; the complete replacement of the complex plate Drag 15/17 by 18 and 18/31; and the eclipse of Drag 29 decorated bowls in favour of the simpler 37 would all seem to indicate this trend. See Hartley (1969, 241-8).

[10] Argonne ware is a partial exception, although never common: see Fulford (1975, 278-9) for example.

[11] In which Silvanus, the *negotiator cretarius* attested amongst the Domburg-Colijnsplaat altars (above, p 43), was presumably involved.

[12] In fairness, the Central Gaulish connections of the Aldgate/Pulborough potter detract from this view (Simpson 1952; Webster 1975).

[13] This and several similar statements relating to trade-routes are included conveniently in Tierney (1960).

References

Albrecht, C, 1939 & 1942   *Das Römerlager in Oberaden*, Veröffentlichungen aus dem Städt Museum für Vor- und Frühgeschichte, Dortmund, **2,** 1 (1939); **2,** 2 (1942).

Atkinson, D, 1914   A hoard of samian ware from Pompeii, *J Roman Stud*, **4,** 27-64.

Boon, G C, 1967   Micaceous sigillata from Lezoux at Silchester, Caerleon, and other sites, *Antiq J*, **47,** 27-42.

Brewster, N H, 1972   Corbridge: its significance for the study of Rhenish ware, *Archaeol Aeliana*, 4 ser, **50,** 205-16.

Bushe-Fox, J P, 1926   *First report on excavations at Richborough, Kent*, Soc Antiquaries Res Rep **6.**

——, 1932   *Third report on excavations at Richborough, Kent*, Soc Antiquaries Res Rep **10.**

Collingwood, R G, & Richmond, I A, 1969   *The archaeology of Roman Britain.*

Cunliffe, B W, 1975   *Excavations at Portchester Castle, I, Roman*, Soc Antiquaries Res Rep **32.**

Curle, J, 1911   *A Roman frontier post and its people; the fort of Newstead in the parish of Melrose.*

Dannell, G B, 1973   The potter Indixivixus, in Detsicas 1973, 139-42.

Detsicas, A P (ed), 1973   *Current research in Romano-British coarse pottery*, CBA Res Rep **10.**

Drexel, F, 1911   Nr 66c. Das Kastell Faimingen, *Obergerm-Raet Limes*, **35.**

Frere, S S, 1972   *Verulamium excavations, I*, Soc Antiquaries Res Rep **28.**

Fulford, M G, 1975   The pottery, in Cunliffe, 1975, 270-367.

Gillam, J P, 1957   Types of Roman coarse pottery vessels in northern Britain, *Archaeol Aeliana*, 4 ser, **35,** 180-251.

Gose, E, 1950   *Gefässtypen der römischen Keramik im Rheinland*, Bonner Jahrbücher, Beiheft **1.**

Greene, K, 1972   *Guide to pre-Flavian fine wares, c AD 40-70.*

——, 1973   The pottery from Usk, in Detsicas 1973, 25-37.

Hartley, B R, 1969   Samian ware or Terra Sigillata, in Collingwood & Richmond 1969, 235-51.

Hull, M R, 1963   *The Roman potters' kilns of Colchester*, Soc Antiquaries Res Rep **21.**

Johns, C M, 1971   *Arretine and samian pottery.*

Lasfargues, J, 1972   Une industrie lyonnaise, *Archéol Trésors Ages*, **50,** 15-19.

Loeschcke, S, 1909   Keramische Funde in Haltern, *Mitt Altertumskomm Westfalen*, **5,** 103-322.

Mayet, F, 1975   *Les Céramiques à Parois Fines dans la Péninsule Ibérique*, Publications du Centre Pierre Paris (ERA 522), **I.**

Moevs, M T M, 1973   *The Roman thin-walled pottery from Cosa*, Memoirs of the American Academy in Rome, **32.**

Oelmann, F, 1914   *Die Keramik des Kastells Niederbieber*, Mater Röm-Germ Keramik.

Oswald, F, & Pryce, T D, 1920   *An introduction to the study of Terra Sigillata* (reprint 1966).

Picon, M, 1973   *Introduction à l'Étude Technique des Céramiques Sigillées de Lezoux.*

Schindler-Kaudelka, E, 1975   *Die dünnwandige Gebrauchskeramik vom Magdalensberg*, Kärntner Museumsschriften, **58.**

Simpson, G, 1952, The Aldgate potter, *J Roman Stud*, **42,** 68-71.

——, 1957   Metallic black slip vases from central Gaul with applied and moulded decoration, *Antiq J*, **37,** 29-42.

——, 1973   More black slip vases from Central Gaul with applied and moulded decoration in Britain, *Antiq J*, **53,** 42-51.

Tierney, J J, 1960   The Celtic ethnography of Posidonius, *Proc Roy Ir Acad*, **60,** 189-275.

Vegas, M, 1969-70   ACO-Becher, *Acta Rei Cretariae Rom Fautorum*, **11-12,** 107-24.

——, 1975   Die augustische Gebrauchskeramik von Neuss, *Novaesium VI*, Limesforschurgen, **14,** 3-76.

Webster, P V, 1975   More British samian ware by the Aldgate-Pulborough potter, *Britannia*, **6,** 163-70.

Young, C J, 1973   The pottery industry of the Oxford region, in Detsicas 1973, 105-15.

Postscript

This paper was completed in March 1977. Since then the writer has undertaken further research in France and Germany which has strengthened the division between Central Gaulish and Trier 'rhenish' ware, by showing that the two categories have almost completely separate distributions (the latter is extremely rare west of the river Saône), and that other production centres between Lezoux and Trier were not likely to have made closely similar wares. In addition, the low-girthed cornice-rimmed beaker form was found to be absent from Central Gaul; this further emphasizes the Rhineland origins of the Nene Valley and Colchester industries, but makes the attribution of Fig 46, no 2, to Central Gaul unlikely. I would like to thank M Desnoyers (Montluçon), J Gourvest (Chateaumeillant), R Albert (Argenton-sur-Creuse), J Corrocher (Vichy), and W Binsfeld (Trier) for their valuable assistance in these researches, which were carried out with the help of a grant from the Research Committee of the University of Newcastle upon Tyne.

A comprehensive account of pre-Flavian colour coated and glazed ware is now in press: K Greene, *Usk excavation report: the pre-Flavian fine wares*, Cardiff—this replaces Greene 1972. For the later fine wares, see K Greene, 'Imported fine wares in Britain to AD 250: a guide to identification', in P Arthur and G Marsh, eds, *Fine wares in early Roman Britain*, Brit Archaeol Rep, forthcoming.

The interpretation of Britain's late Roman trade: the scope of medieval historical and archaeological analogy

Michael Fulford

The evidence provided by pottery for the extent and direction of Britain's late Roman trade has recently been discussed (Fulford 1977). Pottery is certainly the best suited artefact to demonstrate trade and marketing patterns. It is virtually indestructible and excavation produces large amounts of it. Demand for it was sufficient to sustain a considerable number of kilns and the various fabrics can be recognized and characterized with comparative ease. Sources can be identified either by petrology or by comparison with kiln assemblages, sometimes with the assistance of petrology.

As well as pottery, late Roman bronze coins are also found in considerable numbers, but the number of mints supplying Britain with coinage is limited. The three mints of Trier, Lyons, and Arles were the only important sources of coins to Britain and the north-western provinces after 326. Thus, although fluctuations in production at these mints may have economic implications, it is not generally possible to use coins as an accurate index of trade routes and the changes in their relative importance.

Besides pottery and coins, it seems fairly certain that we can recognize other artefacts which crossed the Channel to and from Britain. Pewter and jet were undoubtedly exported, while metal objects like silver plate, glass, and silk were surely imported. None of these can be used to demonstrate the direction and changing volume of trade. Not only do they not survive in quantity, but characterization of sources and recognition of manufacturing centres are also fraught with difficulties.

The concern of this paper is to determine how far it is possible to estimate the scale of Britain's late Roman trade. To this end the archaeological evidence for the Roman period will be compared with that for the medieval period. The latter will then be measured against the documentary evidence for medieval trade. Provided that there is sufficient correspondence between the archaeology of each period, the medieval evidence may then be used as a control by which the performance of late Roman trade may be judged.

In summarizing first the ceramic evidence of trade between Britain and the rest of the empire between the late 3rd and early 5th century attention should be paid to three main types of imported pottery (Fig 48) (Fulford 1977). Precise date ranges cannot be given as much of the material is from unstratified or residual contexts, but all of it, according to the continental evidence, is confined within the limits described above. What dated contexts there are are slightly biased towards the second half of the 4th century. The commonest imported ware is that from the Argonne region of northern France (Chenet 1941; Hübener 1968). It is a red-slipped tableware frequently decorated with roller-stamped designs. Like the British red-slipped wares from the Nene Valley, Oxfordshire, and the New Forest, it can be regarded as the 4th century successor to the early imperial Gaulish red-slipped or samian tradition. In 1975 over 120 examples were known from some 28 sites in England and Wales; one sherd was also found in a Viking context in Dublin. The figures are conservative because, while decorated pieces are readily identifiable, plain sherds can be easily mistaken as late 2nd to 3rd century East Gaulish samian.

The second most important pottery import has a rough coarse fabric whose petrology points to a source in the Eifel Mountains in Germany (Fulford & Bird 1975). This is the late Roman Mayen ware which has a wide distribution along the Rhine and into Switzerland in the 4th century. So far over 90 examples have been recognized from at least 22 sites in Britain. Further examples of this fabric are certain to be identified soon, as excavators become aware of the possibility of its presence in Britain.

The third major imported ware has also only recently been recognized for what it is on British sites. It is described as 'céramique dite à l'éponge' because of its distinctive marbled and 'marigold-patterned' slip. On the basis of its distribution a source has been suggested between the Loire and the Gironde in south-western France (Raimbault 1973). Owing to excavators' unfamiliarity with it, the 36 examples that have been recognized from eighteen sites are likely to be an underestimate of the total number already excavated.

In addition to the common imports there are three others to be considered exclusive of amphorae. Two further German or Rhenish fabrics are known from south-eastern Britain. One is a sandy coarse ware represented by forms similar to those in the Mayen fabric; it has been found on three sites (Fulford & Bird 1975, 173). The second is known from one site only and is a jug with a marbled slip (Gose 1950, type 262 from Swan Street, Southwark). Thirdly, examples of North African red-slipped ware have now been recognized in Roman contexts as well as on post-Roman sites (Bird 1977). So far sherds have been found on six sites of the late, but not necessarily post-Roman, period. As with plain Argonne ware forms, confusion with Gaulish or British red-slipped wares is likely to have limited recognition. Finds of amphorae that carried olive oil from North Africa in later 3rd to 5th century contexts also increase the range of fabrics and areas in trade contact with Britain at this date (Peacock 1977).

Besides imports there are also pottery exports from Britain in the late Roman period (Fig 49). Recognition of these is also recent and so, while an extensive area of Holland, Belgium, and north-western France has been scoured for finds, much more will surely come to light as excavators become familiar with British ceramics. The fine Oxfordshire ware (Young 1973) and the coarse black-burnished ware manufactured in south-east Dorset (Farrar 1973; Williams 1977) are the two most important exports to the continent. The former was Britain's largest source of tableware and the main competitor with Argonne pottery. It has now been identified on eight or nine continental sites with about 20 examples. The second, a coarser kitchen ware, has been found on eight sites and is represented by some 30 sherds. In addition, two pieces of New Forest pottery (Fulford 1975) have been definitely recognized at the site of Alet in Brittany and more than ten sherds of grey kitchen wares identical to those manufactured in southern Britain have been found at three sites. The

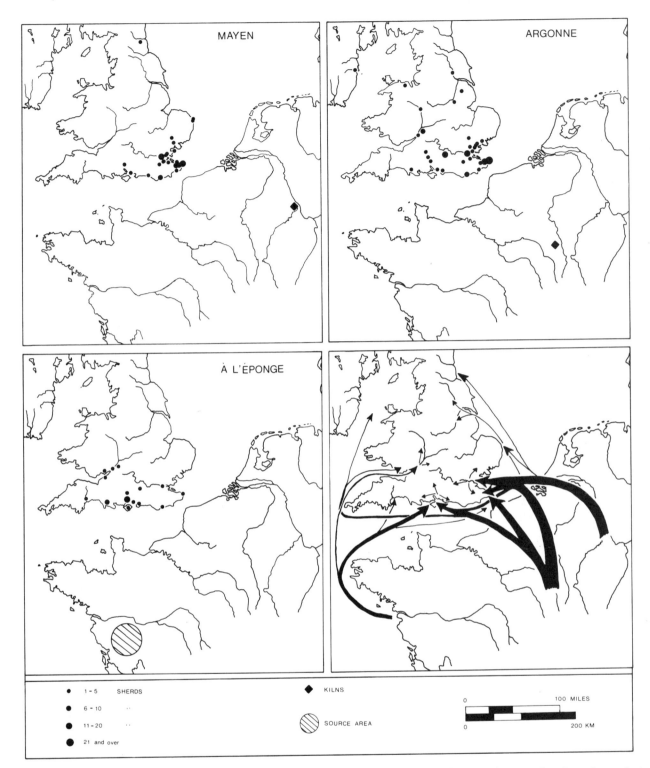

Fig 48   Distribution of pottery imported into late Roman Britain from the continent, showing the relative importance of the main sources and probable trade routes

most likely source for most of these pieces is the Alice Holt-Farnham group of kilns (cf Fulford 1975, 85-8).

Finds of pottery demonstrate that there was a wide range of contacts between Britain and the continent as well as the Mediterranean during the late Roman period. All that remains is to demonstrate or attempt to demonstrate what the picture provided by the archaeology may mean in terms of the actual volume and directions of late Roman trade. Unlike the medieval period there are few

records (and those that exist seldom quantify) which describe the nature of commerce in perishable commodities or in goods whose source may not be readily identifiable or characterizable. The occasional references to British flocks or British wool in panegyrics and Diocletian's Price Edict are only of use to demonstrate that they were appreciated outside Britain (Wild 1970). There is no means of establishing whether wool or cloth might have represented 1% or 90% of British exports.

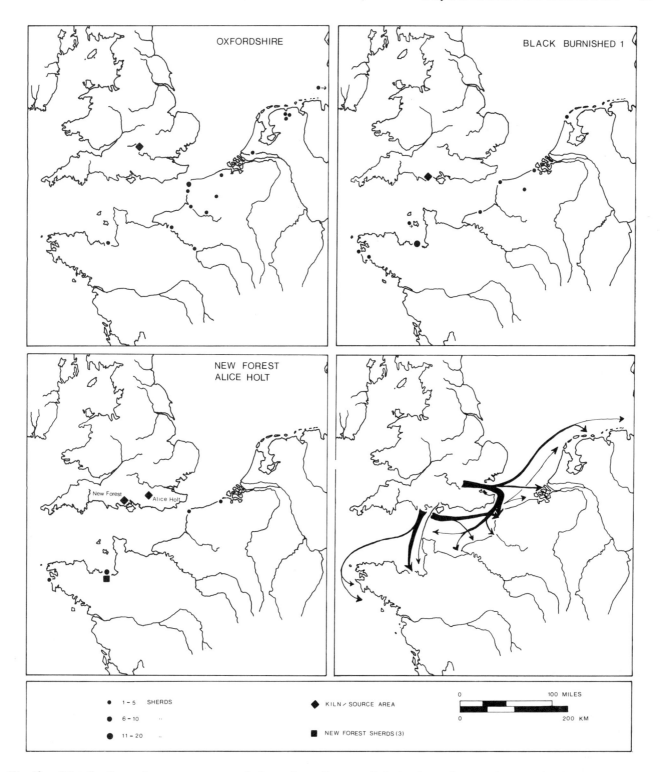

Fig 49 Distribution of pottery exported from late Roman Britain into the continent, showing the relative importance of the main sources and probable trade routes

In comparison with the early Empire, the number of different items that can be shown to have crossed the Channel in the late Roman period is slight, yet even in the early Empire there is only a little more written or epigraphic evidence on the subject of trade. Some might argue that the almost total neglect of economic affairs by Roman writers is a fair reflection of the role of trade in the Roman economy (Finley 1973). Such a view cannot really be substantiated, but it should be pointed out that the early Empire was a period of prosperity as commerce exploited the potential of new markets provided by the expanding Roman world, although contemporary documentation of trade is little better than for the late Empire. Traditionally, of course, the Roman senatorial class washed its hands of business matters and it is likely that such attitudes, sometimes with a legislative basis (*Lex Claudia* in Livy XXI, 63), discouraged much literary expression on economic affairs (Rougé 1966, 11-22).

In returning to the primary archaeological evidence of trade, it must first be established how far changing quantities and distributions of traded items that survive archaeologically actually relate to a real changing pattern and scale of trade. Such an assessment will obviously affect the way the late Roman evidence is interpreted. One of the striking features of the province of Britain during the early Empire is the gradual decline of imports relative to home-produced goods from a peak in the pre-Flavian period. An immediate reaction might be that there was progressive decline in long-distance trade from the early conquest period. This would be nonsense because, firstly, finished goods probably represented only a small proportion of the total volume of trade and, secondly, the apparent decline only correlates with the expansion of British producers. As the demand for Roman consumer articles increased in Britain, it became increasingly uncompetitive to import when equally serviceable items could be manufactured at lower cost within the province. Apparently declining trade is no more than a reflection of the developing romanization of Britain. One cannot entirely rule out some decline in the volume of trade, but on the other hand, as the province settled down under Roman administration, it is likely that the productivity of the island increased, being reflected in the greater export of food and minerals. Strabo's list of British exports at the beginning of the 1st century AD includes corn, cattle, gold, silver, iron, hides, slaves, and hounds. Of these, only the export of minerals *might* be detected in the archaeological record. There is no reason why the export of these should not have increased nor why imports of items also irrecoverable in normal archaeological conditions should not have done likewise during the peaceful era of the 2nd century. Evidence of textiles and wine imported by barrel, both major items of trade in the medieval period, can only be recovered in exceptional circumstances.

In the late Roman period it is reasonable to argue that there was a kind of 'cultural' equilibrium between Britain and the other provinces of the Empire. Consequently the character of the province's overseas trade will be more limited to exchanges not of manufactured goods but of commodities and raw materials which were surplus in one province but scarce in another. A surplus of lead or iron from Britain might be traded for wine from Gaul. In fact a healthy trade in perishables and raw materials could well have been carried on without leaving any trace in the archaeological record. Although metals have a good survival record, analytical techniques are not so advanced that sources can be easily identifiable. The latter need not bear any relation to the location of workshops or the distribution of the finished articles.

In trying to fill in the bare bones of late Roman trade, the documentary evidence for medieval trade will surely prove an invaluable aid, because it provides the necessary control of the archaeological data that is so clearly lacking in the Roman period. From the later 13th century onwards there is a considerable amount of documentation concerning England's overseas trade. Most of the documents are concerned with the duties paid on the import of wine and the export of wool and later cloth (Carus-Wilson & Coleman 1963). In addition certain ports have documents recording the whole composition of cargoes, particularly in the later 14th and 15th centuries. While commodities like wine and wool invited national or royal dues, individual ports were eventually allowed to raise particular customs on all cargoes handled by them in order to maintain the upkeep of wharves and the port generally. Here one not only gains an insight into the character and diversity of cargoes but also into the quantities that were shipped and the numbers of vessels involved in the trading activities of a single port during a given period. Correlation with the trade of the Roman period lies through a comparison of the archaeological evidence for trade in each period.

As will be seen, the archaeological evidence for trade in the medieval period is of a similar character to that of late Roman trade because the same kinds of artefacts survive in roughly the same quantities. As for the Roman period, pottery is the most abundant archaeological fossil with which to document patterns of trade in the middle ages. Other classes of object do survive, such as coins, glass, metal goods, or materials like stone, but invariably in smaller amounts or in circumstances where quantification and source characterization are difficult.

Assuming comparability between the archaeological evidence of trade in each period, it is reasonable to suppose that the character and scale of Roman trade may be illuminated by reference to the documented sources for medieval trade. Although there are great differences between Romano-British and medieval society, these should not necessarily affect a comparative study based on the relationship between archaeological data and documentary sources. The colonizing aspect of trade between Britain and the rest of the empire had died out by the 3rd century, whereafter the essential character of the trade—exporting surplus raw materials and commodities in exchange for goods not available in Britain—was similar to that in the medieval period. Manufactured goods in both periods are not really significant items (see below, pp 67-8). This is not to say that the materials of trade or the direction of trade were necessarily the same, but that overall comparability in the archaeological record suggests the same in the volume of the real trade.

It is now necessary to outline the equivalent pottery evidence for medieval trade. The substance of this is based on Dunning's major paper on trade and medieval pottery prepared in 1966 (1968). This paper was based on some 30 years' research and is now ten years old. Although more sites with imported pottery types and a greater variety of fabrics will undoubtedly have been identified, it nevertheless provides a useful framework with which to compare the Roman material, which has itself only been comprehensively studied over the last five to ten years.

For the 12th century the main imported pottery types are the red-painted wares from Normandy and the Lower Rhineland (Pingsdorf) series (Hurst 1969). The former had been recognized by Dunning at 26 sites in Britain and the latter at nine. Of lesser importance is Andenne ware which is widely distributed in Holland and Belgium and in 1966 was known from two British sites. Regarding exports, it seems that examples of Stamford ware were known from only the one site of Bryggen in Norway.

Thus for the 12th century we have evidence of two major imported pottery types, although there are reasons to suppose that these were the products of more than two kiln groups within the areas of concentrated distribution on the continent. As with the Roman wares, it is difficult to assign close date brackets to these imports. In the case of the red-painted wares, importation was taking place from the 10th century.

For the 13th and early 14th centuries there is a much more varied archaeological picture of trade contact between Britain and Europe which probably reflects a real increase in trade, particularly in the second half of the 13th and the early 14th century. The documentary evidence also suggests an increase in trade, but this may only reflect the greater survival of documentation from the later 13th century. The two most important groups are from Normandy and the Saintonge region of south-western France. The Normandy wares for which kiln centres are not known yet have been found at 26 sites in England and on one site in Wales. Dunning mentions that there are numerous finds in London and at Stonar in Kent, but the incidence per site is not otherwise described. For the south-western French imports Dunning divided the pottery into the polychrome types which he dated to *c* 1275-*c* 1310 and the green-glazed types which appear to span a longer period, continuing through the 14th century. Thirty-four sites in England, nine in Wales, two in Scotland, and three in Ireland have produced examples of the polychrome wares. Large amounts have been noted at London, Southampton, Bristol, and Stonar, which were major entry points for the French wine trade. Of the green-glazed variety, 26 sites in England, six in Wales, and two in Ireland have produced examples. The distribution pattern corresponds closely with that of the polychromes. However, it should be stressed that failure to recognize English copies of French imports may have had an inflationary effect on the figures. Other imported types that have been recognized include three groups whose source seems to be in Holland: Aardenburg pottery has been noted at three sites in Norfolk and Kent, while examples of Zeeland and Bergen op Zoom ware have been found at Dover and Stonar. Kilns have not been located for any of these wares. Rhenish stone-wares have not been included here as they only start to appear at the end of the 14th century (Biddle 1963; Platt & Coleman-Smith 1975).

On the export side, two major types that are found on the continent are Grimston and Scarborough ware. Kilns for the former are known near King's Lynn and at least eleven examples of this type have been recognized on five sites in Norway, Denmark, and the Netherlands. Scarborough ware, for which kilns are not yet known, was found on five sites in Norway and the Netherlands. Knight jugs, which form a typological group, though known to have been made in at least four centres, have also been found on five continental sites. The Surrey wares that provided the major part of London's pottery in the 13th and 14th centuries have been found on four sites in North Germany and the Netherlands and probably represent trade out of London itself. Two other instances of exported pottery might also be mentioned: a Wessex-type baluster jug was found in Holland and coarse wares, probably from London or East Anglia, have been recognized in Bergen.

In summary, the ceramic evidence for medieval trade indicates the following. During the 12th century there were two areas which supplied the bulk of the imports. Basing estimates on the number of sites producing imported sherds, it would seem that Normandy provided about 70% of imports, while the figure for the Lower Rhineland is about 25%. As no characterization studies have yet been made of the red-painted wares in Britain, too much weight should not be placed on the attribution to sources. For the later 13th to 14th century there were again two main areas supplying Britain's imports: Normandy and the Saintonge region of south-western France. Between them they accounted for about 95% of the trade. The Saintonge products are relatively more important than those from Normandy.

Ceramic exports from Britain are of little importance in the 12th century. In the 13th and 14th century seven classes of ware (not necessarily seven fabrics) were traded to the continent. Grimston ware and Scarborough ware seem to have been the most important; with Surrey ware and the knight jugs about 80% of the finds are accounted for.

Comparison between the medieval and the late Roman period is immediately attractive. During the latter there were three main sources of imports compared with only two in the 13th-14th century. With exports there were again two important components accounting for nearly 80% of the finds in the 3rd-4th century. If all classes are considered, irrespective of the number of finds, there are five late Roman imports (excluding Mediterranean wares) to four or five medieval (also excluding Mediterranean and Spanish wares), while there are four exported wares to seven of the 13th-14th century. The two more important late Roman exported types are known from more sites and in greater numbers than any of the equivalent medieval varieties.

Admittedly these figures are rough and ready and they should be tested against a programme of characterization and comparison with kiln assemblages. English copies of medieval imports, for example, may reduce the overall level of imports in that period. Nevertheless, given the quality of the data, there seems to be reasonable comparability between the late Roman trade as represented by pottery finds spread over 150 years and that of the later 13th to 14th century, which represents a similar time-span. Immediately striking is the lack of comparability between the 12th century and the late Roman period. Thus, if there is a correlation between the scale of trade in pottery in each period and the real volume of trade, it would seem that the documentary evidence of the late 13th to 14th century trade would give a better idea of the nature and volume of late Roman trade than the rather scanty historical evidence for the character of 12th century trade.

So far the evidence considered has been concerned only with the trade between those countries or provinces that border the North Sea and the Channel (as well as Gascony/Aquitaine). Pottery of both periods also documents a longer-distance trade between Britain and Spain and the Mediterranean. Small quantities of North African red-slipped wares are known in Britain from the late Roman period (see above, p 59). African oil-carrying amphorae have also been found in late 3rd to 4th century contexts in Britain (see above, p 59). Other Mediterranean fabrics of this date include micacaceous water jars (Biv type, as defined in Thomas 1959) from the Aegean or other eastern source. Similarly, from the late 13th century there is evidence of pottery imports from Spain and definite Italian wares from the early 14th century in Southampton (Platt & Coleman-Smith 1975). In both periods finds of this kind are very rare and in general are restricted to port or urban contexts.

Clearly, much more reliable comparisons could be made between the ceramic evidence of the two periods if there were more figures for the ratio of imports to indigenous wares. During the late Roman period individual categories of import can scarcely account for even 1% of the total pottery assemblage. Exceptions might be Argonne ware and the German coarse (Mayen) pottery from London and south-eastern counties like Essex and Kent, where large numbers have already been recognized (as at Richborough). There is also a spread of finds on rural sites, few of which can be considered as rich settlements. Nevertheless, rough estimates at Canterbury and Richborough, for example, where assemblages no longer survive in their original state, do not indicate that late Roman imports ever amounted to more than 10% of assemblages. '*A l'éponge ware*' at Clausentum also suggests no greater representation than 5% of the total assemblage (Fulford 1977).

In the medieval period there seems to be a similar situation, except at major ports like Bristol, London, and Southampton. As in the Roman period, the majority of excavated sites in Britain have produced no evidence of imports at all. In other cases the total proportion of foreign imports very rarely exceeds 1%. At Bristol (Baldwin Street), for example, Rahtz (1960, 236) estimated that nearly 14% of the sherds were imported. At a site on the Castle Wall a similar figure of 13% was obtained for the imports (Barton 1959). A third site in the city, however, only produced 1% in imports (Barton 1960). From the smaller port of Dover one group of pottery from the mid-13th century produced nearly 25% of its pottery from Norman and south-western French sources (Rix & Dunning 1955). A second group from the same port and dating from the late 13th century had by contrast no recognizable imports. Yet another pit group, also of the late 13th to early 14th century, contained fifteen vessels of which a quarter were imported (Rigold 1967). Southampton offers a similar picture, although Platt and Coleman-Smith only provide details of a limited number of pit groups (1975). The average proportion of imported ware is about 25% during the 13th and 14th centuries. The pit with the lowest figure had 6%, while that with the highest had 50%. Apart from London, which also looks as if it will produce high figures (Thorn 1974), there are other occasional instances of high percentages of imports in comparatively small groups, as at Lesnes Abbey (Dunning 1961) and Waterbeach (Cra'ster 1966).

Overall, the pattern of evidence suggests a low-density inland distribution with concentrations at ports of entry. In many cases, as at Southampton, there may be a direct association between large proportions of imports and the documented presence of resident foreign merchants. That a factor of this kind may have been responsible is suggested by the variation from group to group at the three ports discussed above. Royal and aristocratic households as well as certain monastic foundations are perhaps to be regarded as greater consumers of exotic wares than the lower classes. However, few of these sites have been extensively excavated and the site of King John's Hunting Lodge at Writtle, Essex, which only produced sherds of four imported vessels dating before the 16th century, may not be exceptional (Rahtz 1969). A further explanation for the larger concentration and higher percentages of imports at the ports when compared with the later Roman period may be that inland marketing was less efficient in the 13th and 14th centuries than it was during the Roman administration.

Such a suggestion may be substantiated by comparing the general patterns of pottery marketing in each period. During the late Roman period there were two major producers of fine tableware pottery, one in Oxfordshire, the other in the Nene Valley. While the former commanded a very extensive market over southern England (including the south midlands), accounting for between 5% and 25% of pottery assemblages and seldom absent at any site (cf Fulford & Hodder 1975), the latter marketed large amounts of its products over central England, with an additional market in the military zone of northern Britain. Finds have also been found at large numbers of sites outside the main distribution area, but in quantities of less than 5% and usually as occasional sherds. Oxfordshire ware is found as far north as southern Scotland and Nene Valley sherds have been recognized south of the Thames.

In addition to the two kiln groups with almost province-wide distributions, mention also ought to be made of the New Forest kilns which supplied much of the pottery demand in central southern England in direct competition with the Oxfordshire kilns. Furthermore, there were several large centres manufacturing more utilitarian vessels, like cooking pots, with very extensive distributions. Late Roman black-burnished ware of a southern Dorset origin is found over much of the province, with special emphasis in the south. The extended nature of the distribution to Hadrian's Wall may partly be explained by the military presence there, but until the proportion of this fabric to others all over the province is known, it will not be possible to say whether there is an unusually large amount on military sites. Nevertheless, there are superficial similarities in the distribution with that of the medieval Saintonge ware which also is found in military contexts on Welsh and Scottish castle sites. Kilns near Farnham and in the Alice Holt Forest supplied a similar range of utilitarian wares to the south-east and account for up to 50% of the pottery present on late Roman sites in London. The marketing pattern of these kilns may prove similar to, or even more extensive than, that of the medieval Surrey wares which formed a large component of the pottery supplied to London (M Lyne, pers comm).

There are some examples of late Roman wares which can be shown to have been marketed over extensive areas of Britain and at the same time to account for at least 5% and often much more of the relevant assemblages. In contrast, the evidence for the medieval marketing of pottery is not nearly so impressive. There are no known pottery types or fabrics which have more than a regional or extended county distribution. The Surrey wares, the West Sussex wares, and the Wessex type jugs of the 13th to 14th century are good examples of pottery marketed over a limited area. In Yorkshire, too, pottery seems to have been produced at a number of local centres to be sold locally (Bellamy & le Patourel 1970). Individual kiln centres are not known on anything like the same scale as their late Roman predecessors. None have left the extensive waste heaps that are the mark of the Roman New Forest and Alice Holt kilns. It is not until Tudor green wares appear towards the end of the 14th century that one has evidence of pottery beginning to reach a wide market on, say, the scale of late Roman Oxfordshire ware. Tudor green does not, of course, achieve its greatest popularity until the 15th century.

Admittedly a large programme of characterization needs to be initiated on medieval pottery with quantitative analyses of site assemblages, but even in the present state of knowledge there seems to be a distinct difference in the efficiency of the late Roman market in comparison with that of the medieval period. Thus, while imported wares seem to be represented overall as a greater percentage of pottery assemblages at ports than is the case in the Roman period, this need not reflect on the overall level of trade. Social factors, like the presence of alien merchants or the ineffectiveness of inland marketing, may be the explanation. In fact the medieval evidence up to the end of the 14th century may be argued to show that the level of late Roman trade was superior to that of England until the 15th century.

So far no check has been applied to the medieval pottery evidence of trade to see how it corresponds with other categories of archaeological material and the documented evidence of trade. In comparison with imported pottery, which shows an overwhelming bias towards the south-west of France as the main source area, foreign coins in British hoards for the 13th and 14th centuries are mostly from the Low Countries and the Rhineland (Thompson 1956). Unlike the Roman Empire, where coins circulated freely between the provinces, in the medieval period coins were not always accepted as legal tender outside the state which minted them. However, a small number of foreign coins does occur in hoards deposited in the British Isles during the 13th and 14th centuries, but seldom accounting for more than 1% of the hoard. The proportion of hoards (taking account only of those reasonably recorded) with foreign coins rises from 31% in the 13th century to 83% in the following hundred years. The majority of coins in both centuries are from Belgium and the Netherlands (Flanders, Hainaut, Namur, Brabant, Luxembourg, Lorraine, Bar, Cambrai, Porcien, and the Holy Roman Empire). Only a tiny proportion of those coins deposited in hoards were struck in the Anglo-Gallic territory of Aquitaine from which most of the imported wine and pottery originated.

Historical evidence indicates that the export trade between Britain and Flanders was of the utmost importance, greater than that with Gascony (Carus-Wilson & Coleman 1963). This situation is not supported by the pottery evidence. There are few British sherds in the Low Countries and few imports from that region so far recognized in Britain. Although there is agreement between the coins and the documented record, the former, because of their scarcity, particularly outside of hoard contexts, do not allow much opportunity for demonstrating detailed marketing patterns and trade routes in the way that pottery does. The south-western French imports, on the other hand, do support the historical evidence for the supremacy of Gascony in the wine trade in the 14th and 15th centuries (James 1971).

For the Roman period it is also possible to contrast the ceramic evidence for trade with that provided by coins. However, whereas the medieval coin find is usually of silver (there being no lower denominational coin) the common Roman coin find is of bronze. While a discussion of the value of coinage for demonstrating economic behaviour has been made elsewhere (Fulford, forthcoming), it is necessary to summarize a few points here. After the closure of the London mint in 326 the three operating at Trier, Lyons, and Arles respectively supplied the bulk of Britain's coinage. In the earlier part of the 4th century Trier had had the most important mint, but gradually its supremacy was eroded by Arles and Lyons (Fig 50). The question arises as to how far the shift in emphasis from the north to the southern pair reflects a conscious political decision to move the source of coin supply regardless of the source of the demand and how far it is connected with changes in economic conditions outside the control of imperial policy. In essence it is argued that the second premise has more support from a quantitative study of coin assemblages and that the latter do suggest a genuine switch in the emphasis of Britain's overseas trade to the south of Gaul and the Mediterranean in the second half of the 4th century. Some support for this is provided by the finds of North African amphorae and tablewares, but these only account for a minute proportion of Britain's total late Roman imports. Paradoxically, like the medieval

situation, the coin evidence does not really correlate with the pottery. The bulk of Britain's imports are from the Rhineland and northern France, while most of the exports have been found in the latter area and the Low Countries. Moreover the greater proportion of the dated contexts of imports proves to lie in the second half of the 4th century, when the source of coin is shifting to the south. Late Roman coins, while comparatively plentiful, are not so useful in demonstrating particular trade routes and market patterns because of the limited number of sources. In conclusion it may be stated that while the evidence of pottery can be used to demonstrate the existence of trade links, the greater abundance of one type rather than another cannot necessarily be used as evidence of the relative importance of the source areas in the volume of real trade, which is largely concealed in the archaeological record. The evidence for the medieval period *may* encourage the view that the order of importance of the archaeologically established trade-routes does not closely resemble that of the actual trade.

Further comparison of the scale of trade between the two periods may be made by examining ship and cargo sizes. The typical ship of the medieval period was the cog. Size varied considerably, but 200 tons burden* seems to have been the maximum in the 13th century and such ships were designed for the longer journeys. In the 13th century some cogs were built of 400-500 tons burden but these were rare (Carr Loughton 1960). Some details of ships trading out of Bristol in the 14th century are recorded which show that vessels of 100 tons burden were the most common, but that ships of 200 tons burden were not uncommon. From the middle of the 15th century there were a greater proportion of vessels of 200-300 tons. William of Canynges had ten ships in his fleet of which seven were of 220 tons, one of 500 tons, and an exceptional ship of 900 tons. In 1480 at Bristol there is a record of eight vessels registered at about 200 tons, five at about 100 tons, and two of 300 and 360 tons respectively. The sizes of coastal vessels is not well documented as customs dues were not required for cargoes of English origin. However, in 1513 all but one of the vessels recorded in the port at one time were of less than 130 tons (Sherborne 1965).

Northern England provides another interesting insight into shipping at the end of the 13th century (Conway Davies 1953). In 1294 55 ships took shelter from a winter storm at Newcastle-upon-Tyne, Scarborough, and Ravenspur and, as they hailed from ports unfriendly to England at the time, their cargoes were confiscated. Of the 21 vessels for which details survive, three were of 30 tons burden, seven of 40 tons, four of 50, five of 60 tons, one of 70, and one of 100 tons burden. It is difficult to be certain whether the storm only affected the smaller ships at sea at the time, but they give some indication of the scale of shipping at that date. In conclusion it would seem that in the 13th century vessels over 100 tons were rare, while in the 14th it was ships over 200 tons that were uncommon. In the 15th century ships over 200 tons were not unusual.

For the later Roman Empire we have to rely mostly on literary sources for information about ship sizes. Calculating tonnage from either literary evidence or the remains of wrecks presents problems and any modern conversion figure must be regarded as tentative (cf

---

*Ship size has been based on cargo capacity. Lane estimated 1 ton burden as about 1 metric tonne (Lane 1965a).

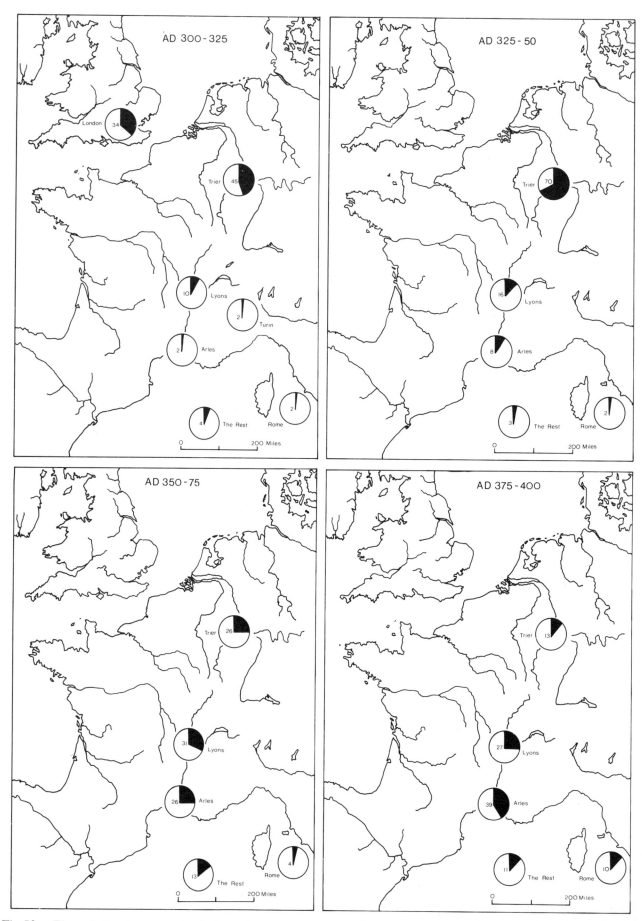

Fig 50   The relative importance of the mints supplying Britain with bronze coinage through the 4th century. The percentages represent the average from six large British site collections (Fulford, forthcoming)

Rougé 1966, 66-71; Casson 1971, 183-200; Lane 1965a). A few wrecks of the period have been excavated efficiently, among which the late 3rd century wreck of 60 tons burden from the County Hall site in London should be noted (Marsden 1972, 116-18). From the Mediterranean the 6th century stone-carrying Marzamemi ship was about 300 tons burden, while the Yassi Ada wrecks of the 4th and 7th centuries respectively seem to have carried cargoes of less than 100 tons burden (Throckmorton 1972, 72-6; Van Doorninck 1972, 136-46). With the redirection of the Egyptian corn supply to Constantinople instead of Rome, ship sizes tended to decrease as the distances to be covered correspondingly lessened. Indeed, the government thought it worthwhile to charter ships of 2000 modii (about 15 tons burden) (Jones 1964, 843). Earlier, under the Principate, vessels engaged in the corn supply had had to carry a minimum cargo of 75 tons burden (Gaius 1.32). Belisarius's invasion fleet of AD 533 contained 500 vessels for the invasion of Africa and none of these was of less than 150 tons burden (Procopius, BV 1.xi, 13). Elsewhere John of Moschus (d 620) refers to a ship of 230 tons as exceptionally large, because of the difficulty involved in launching it. In another passage John implies that a ship of 330 tons burden was exceptional (*Pratum Spirituale*, 83, 190).

From these scanty references it may be supposed that vessels up to 200 tons were common in the late Empire. This would compare well with the state of shipping in northern waters in the 14th century. However it is by no means certain that the ships designed for the North Sea and the Atlantic in the late Roman period were built to the same size as those that plied the Mediterranean. There is no inherent reason why there should be a difference, particularly as the northern seas required more rugged vessels and ships below a certain size would have been vulnerable in high seas. However, a check can be made with the renaissance period, when it can be shown that the sizes of merchant vessels built in Venice were not significantly different from their contemporaries in Britain (Lane 1965b, 33-50, 222-23). If such was the case in the 15th and 16th centuries, there is no reason to suppose any difference in the 13th and 14th centuries.

If one accepts, then, a broad degree of comparability in the scale of trade in the late Roman and medieval periods on the basis of the archaeological evidence, further use of the medieval documentary evidence may helpfully illuminate the character of the earlier, Roman commerce. The most important early medieval export was wool, which was later replaced more and more by the export of cloth. In return England imported cloth or clothing and wine from Gascony. Surveys of the changing pattern of the English wooltrade and the import of wine have been made on the basis of the custom paid on the former and the King's Prise exacted from cargoes of the latter. It need not be stressed that neither of these commodities necessarily leaves any trace in the archaeological record. In the Roman period both commodities are likely also to have formed an appreciable component of trade. Diocletian's Edict and the panegyricists indicate the possible importance of British wool and woollens (see p 60). Wine was an important import in the early Empire which can be measured; the main source was the Mediterranean and the containers were amphorae made of fired clay. In the later Empire it was natural that the bulk of Britain's wine should be bought from the newly developed and more accessible vineyards in Gaul and the Rhineland. The most convenient container from the more temperate

climate was the barrel, as contemporary funeral monuments seem to indicate (cf Neumagen Sculpture in Wightman 1970, pl 16a). Barrels were rarely marked, even to reveal their contents; they seldom survive in the archaeological record (Ulbert 1959).

Although wool, textiles, and wine might have accounted for the bulk of the trade between Britain and the rest of the empire, other goods were also involved. It may be possible to learn from medieval documentary evidence something of the character of the rest of the cargoes. Fortunately, although few lists of entire cargoes survive before the 15th century, at Southampton there exist two tables of customs dues that were to be paid on goods entering harbour. One of these lists dates to c 1300, the other to 1329 (Studer 1910-11). There are about 130 items which can be broken down into eleven classes: alcoholic beverages, such as wine, cider, and beer; fish; skins such as leather, hides, and furs; wool; wood; manufactured hardwares; cloth; minerals and metals; agricultural produce; spices; stone. Of these only stone, minerals, and manufactured goods incorporating non-perishable materials might survive in the archaeological record in the normal way. The manufactured articles include a 'horse load of Battery' (probably kitchen utensils of brass and copper), the hauberk or haubergeon (a sleeveless coat/jacket of mail), tin, copper, brass, lead (all as unworked metal), millstones, slates, a group of drinking cups, basins, plates and saucers, and a cart. Out of those that might survive or partially survive, the sources of the slates and millstones might be closely identified and the fabric of the crockery might be readily characterized, but none of the other objects would necessarily be recognizable as foreign imports unless there were distinctive typological features about them. The unworked metal ingots might be very difficult to trace to a particular source, especially as the chances of finding examples in an 'as shipped' state would not be good. The evidence of archaeology, then, in the case of the commodities shipped in to Southampton at the beginning of the 14th century, would normally only reveal conclusive evidence of a tiny fragment of that trade. The later list of the two does not add any item, except haberdashery, which *might* be recognizable amongst excavated finds.

A similar unrepresentative situation can be demonstrated at Bristol (Carus-Wilson 1937). Between 1323 and 1325 the surviving records show that of the eleven cargoes carried by alien ships on which duty had to be paid, none would normally survive in the archaeological record. Better accounts survive for the late 14th century when the subsidy was collected on goods going in and out of the port. Of 66 cargoes listed for 1378-79 evidence of eleven, or perhaps twelve, which contained quantities of iron, might survive the passage of time. Whether the iron could be related to a source is another matter. The cargoes listed for 1437 and 1461 indicate a similar frequency of non-perishable cargoes, all of which were of iron. For 1479-80 when 191 sailings were listed, only sixteen included cargoes of this sort, out of which all but three contained iron or coal. The three included combs, shears, and girdles which may or may not have been distinctive from their English counterparts. One immediately impressive point to emerge from the customs lists is that the entire trade between Bristol and Ireland would leave no trace in the archaeological record.

In the 15th century at Southampton port books covering both the alien and denizen trade provide a more detailed picture of traffic through the port. In 1435-36 the contents of 93 cargoes on which duty was paid are listed (Foster 1963). Forty-seven cargoes contained a proportion of non-perishable items, but only twenty contained manufactured articles that might be readily identifiable on typological or analytical grounds. The other 27 merely carried unworked tin, iron, lead, and coal. With the alien ships (usually of Italian origin) three-quarters of the twenty cargoes listed contained non-perishables, but only one-quarter included objects that might be readily identifiable.

It should be stressed that with very few exceptions cargoes were not limited in the range of goods carried. Exclusive cargoes were almost entirely limited to slate and wine. Similar diversity in cargoes seems also to have been the case in the Roman period. Although *negotiatores* specializing in certain commodities like salt, wine, or even pottery are known, there is little evidence that vessels carried only one type of cargo. Ships engaged in the corn supply *may* be exceptional in this respect. No cargo lists, of course, survive but careful wreck excavation has shown diversity in the cargo, even among the few articles that are not destroyed (cf Liou 1973). Pottery itself seldom appears among the port book lists. In 1439-40 at Southampton out of more than 400 cargoes on which customs dues were paid, one alone contained glass and possibly some pottery (two barrels of plates) (Cobb 1961, 11). A second carried pots and pans but these were more likely to have been of brass than pottery. The earlier port book of 1435-36 has one reference to a cargo which had four dozen painted pots and to three others carrying jars of oil. Thus one of the most important (and least valued) items of trade becomes one of the most important in the archaeological record.

Given that there is comparability in the trade of the two periods in terms of the archaeology, it seems reasonable also to propose that this represents the same proportion of the total real trade of the time. Port books and customs records imply that what in fact survives is less than a fraction of 1% of the original volume of trade. It is difficult to imagine that the finds of the late Roman period could represent the plying of hundreds of ships per year to and from the coasts of Britain. Of what survives of the records of major ports like Bristol and Southampton of the 14th and 15th centuries none suggests less than 100 sailings per annum of ships with customable goods (the figure is often nearer 200). This takes no account of coasting traffic. Equally difficult is to imagine that the archaeological evidence for trade in fact represents the import and export of thousands of tons of goods a year. Wine imports alone in the early 14th century probably totalled about 20,000 tons per annum to England, although in the mid-14th century the annual total had fallen to about 8,000 tons and in 1371-2 the total was as low as 6,000 tons. Improvements followed and by the early 1380s imports of wine again ran at about 14,000 tons per annum and were maintained at about that level until the mid-15th century (James 1971). These figures may give the impression that trade in the medieval period (and hence the late Roman period) played an important part in the economy. The opposite is probably nearer the truth. Although estimates of GNP are extremely difficult to arrive at for the medieval and early modern period, Clarkson (1971, 130) has suggested a figure for England of about £50 millions in 1700, of which exported goods accounted for some £4.4 millions. Thus for the 14th century it is extremely unlikely that exported goods would have accounted for even 5% of

GNP which, as has been suggested, might be comparable to the late Roman situation.

In the present state of knowledge for both the Roman and medieval periods, closely spaced fluctuations in trade cannot be detected from archaeological evidence. It is, however, instructive to see the close correlation between the incidence of war and famine and the downward trend of trade figures. Evidence has elsewhere been assembled to suggest that the trading links of late Roman Britain were initially with the Rhineland and the Low Countries but that these were deflected towards the south of Gaul and the Mediterranean during the second half of the 4th century (Fulford 1977; forthcoming). One of the explanations for this might be sought in the devastation caused by barbarian incursions across the Rhine in the 350s. At the outbreak of the Hundred Years' War in 1337 the French attacked the vineyards of Gascony and harried them for three years, with the direct result that wine exports from Bordeaux fell steeply (James 1971, 15).

In summary it may be suggested that a profitable comparison can be made between the archaeological evidence of trade in the late Roman and medieval periods as far as Britain is concerned. The comparison may be taken to the end of the 14th and perhaps as far as the mid-15th century before the evidence becomes incompatible with that of the late Roman period. The documentary sources of the later historic period then provide a control by which to judge the scale and character of the 'archaeological' trade in the late Roman period. The result puts into perspective traditional views that the late Roman period was a time of limited trade and prosperity. There were clear differences between the early and late Imperial trade where Britain and the north-western provinces were concerned, but the former reflects the cultural inequality between the outer provinces and the romanized heart of the empire in the 1st and 2nd centuries AD, rather than a difference in the total volume of trade.

References

Barton, K J, 1959   A group of medieval jugs from Bristol Castle well, *Trans Bristol Gloucestershire Archaeol Soc*, **78**, 169-74.
——, 1960   Excavations at Back Hall, Bristol, 1958, *ibid*, **79**, 251-86.
Bellamy, C V, & Le Patourel, H E J, 1970   Four medieval pottery kilns on Woodhouse Farm, Winksley, near Ripon, West Riding of Yorkshire, *Medieval Archaeol*, **14**, 104-25.
Biddle, M, 1963   Imports of medieval stone-wares from the Rhineland, *ibid*, **6-7**, 298-300.
Bird, J, 1977   African red slip ware in Roman Britain, in *Roman pottery studies in Britain and beyond: papers presented to J P Gillam* (eds K T Greene & J Dore), 269-78.
Carr Laughton, L G, 1960   The cog, *Mariner's Mirror*, **46**, 69-70.
Carus-Wilson, E M (ed), 1937   *The overseas trade of Bristol*, Bristol Record Society.
Carus-Wilson, E M, & Coleman, O, 1963   *England's export trade 1275-1547*.
Casson, L, 1971   *Ships and seamanship in the ancient world*.
Chenet, G, 1941   *La céramique gallo-romaine d'Argonne du IVe siècle et la terre sigillée décorée à la moulette*.
Clarkson, L A, 1971   *The pre-industrial economy in England, 1500-1750*.
Cobb, H S (ed), 1961   *The local Port Book of Southampton for 1439-40*.
Conway Davies, J, 1953   Shipping and trade in Newcastle-upon-Tyne, 1294-96, *Archaeol Aeliana*, 4 ser, **31**, 175-204.
Cra'ster, M D, 1966   Waterbeach Abbey, *Proc Cambridge Antiq Soc*, **59**, 75-94.
Dunning, G C, 1961   A group of English and imported medieval pottery from Lesnes Abbey, Kent; and the trade in early Hispano-Moresque pottery to England, *Antiq J*, **41**, 1-12.
——, 1968   The trade in medieval pottery around the North Sea, in *Rotterdam Papers: A contribution to medieval archaeology* (ed J G N Renand).

Farrar, R A H, 1973   The techniques and sources of Romano-British black-burnished ware, in *Current research in Romano-British coarse pottery* (ed A Detsicas), CBA Res Rep **10,** 67-103.

Finley, M I, 1973   *The ancient economy*.

Foster, B (ed), 1963   *The local Port Book of Southampton for 1435-36*.

Fulford, M G, 1975   *New Forest Roman pottery: manufacture and distribution with a corpus of pottery types*.

——, 1977   Pottery and Britain's foreign trade in the later Roman period, in *Pottery and early commerce* (ed D P S Peacock), 35-84.

——, forthcoming   Coin circulation and mint activity in the later Roman Empire: some economic implications, *Archaeol J,* **135.**

Fulford, M, & Bird, J, 1975   Imported pottery from Germany in late Roman Britain, *Britannia,* **6,** 171-81.

Fulford, M, & Hodder, I R, 1975   A regression analysis of some late Roman pottery: a case study, *Oxoniensia,* **39,** 28-35.

Gaius   *Institutiones,* in *Fontes Iuris Romani Ante-Iustiniani,* **II,** Florence 1941, 9-192.

Gose, E, 1950   *Gefässtypen der römischen keramik im Rheinland,* Beiheft der *Bonner Jahrbücher*.

Hübener, W, 1968   Eine Studie zur spatrömischen Rädchen-sigillata (Argonnensigillata), *Bonner Jahrbücher,* **168,** 241-98.

Hurst, J G (ed), 1969   Red-painted and glazed pottery in western Europe from the eighth to the twelfth century, *Medieval Archaeol* **13,** 93-147.

James, M K, 1971   (ed E M Veale) *Studies in the medieval wine trade*.

John of Moschus   *Pratum Spirituale,* in *Patrologia Graeca,* **87.** iii, 2851-3112.

Jones, A H M, 1964   *The late Roman Empire AD 284-602*.

Lane, F C, 1965a   Tonnage, medieval and modern, *Econ Hist Rev,* 2 ser, **17,** 213-33.

——, 1965b   *Navires et Constructeurs à Venise pendant la Renaissance*.

Liou, B, 1973   Direction des recherches sous-marines, *Gallia,* **31,** 571-608.

Marsden, P, 1972   Ships of the Roman period and after in Britain, in *A history of sea-faring based on underwater archaeology* (ed G F Bass), 113-32.

Peacock, D P S, 1977   Roman amphorae: typology, fabric and origins, in *Méthodes classiques et méthodes formelles dans l'étude des amphores,* Ecole Franç de Rome, 261-78.

Platt, C P S, & Coleman-Smith, R, 1975   *Excavations in medieval Southampton 1953-1969,* Vol 2, *The finds*.

Procopius of Caesarea   *Bellum Vandalicum,* ed Teubner, 1905-13.

Rahtz, P A, 1960   Excavations by the town wall, Baldwin Street, Bristol, 1957, *Trans Bristol & Gloucestershire Archaeol Soc,* **79,** 221-50.

——, 1969   *Excavations at King John's Hunting Lodge, Writtle, Essex, 1955-57*.

Raimbault, M, 1973   La céramique gallo-romaine dite à l'éponge, *Gallia,* **31,** 185-206.

Rigold, S E, 1967   Excavations at Dover Castle, 1964-1966, *J Brit Archaeol Ass,* 3 ser, **30,** 87-121.

Rix, M M, & Dunning, G C, 1955   Excavation of a medieval garderobe in Snargate Street, Dover, *Archaeol Cantiana,* **69,** 132-58.

Rougé, J, 1966   *Recherches sur l'organisation du commerce maritime en Mediterranée sous l'empire Romain*.

Sherborne, J W, 1965   *The port of Bristol in the middle ages,* Historical Association.

Studer, P (ed), 1910-11   *The Oak Book of Southampton of AD 1300,* Southampton Record Society.

Thomas, C, 1959   Imported pottery in Dark-Age Western Britain, *Medieval Archaeol,* **3,** 89-111.

Thompson, J D A, 1956   *Inventory of British coin hoards AD 600-1500*.

Thorn, J C, 1974   in Excavation at the Custom House Site, City of London 1973 (T Tatton-Brown), *Trans London Middlesex Archaeol Soc,* **25,** 180-2.

Throckmorton, P, 1972   Romans on the sea, in *A history of sea-faring based on underwater archaeology* (ed G F Bass), 65-86.

Ulbert, G, 1959   Römische Holzfässer aus Regensburg, *Bayerische Vorgeschichtsblätter,* **24,** 6-29.

Van Doorninck, F, 1972   Byzantium, Mistress of the Sea: 330-641, in *A history of sea-faring based on underwater archaeology* (ed G F Bass), 133-58.

Wightman, E M, 1970   *Roman Trier and the Treveri*.

Wild, J P, 1970   *Textile manufacture in the northern Roman provinces*.

Williams, D, 1977   Romano-British black-burnished industry, in *Pottery and early commerce* (ed D P S Peacock), 163-220.

Young, C J, 1973   The pottery industry of the Oxfordshire region, in *Current research in Romano-British coarse pottery* (ed A Detsicas), CBA Res Rep **10,** 105-15.

In this paper, the term 'trade' has been taken to mean commercial activity on a considerable scale, and different forms of evidence for such activity in Britain and the Rhineland during the Roman period will be examined.

Glassmaking sites

The first matter for consideration must be the information to be gained from glassmaking sites, as it is of fundamental importance to establish the place of manufacture of an object before its presence at that or a different site can be assessed in terms of trade. Harden pointed out many years ago that there were only three sources of 'incontrovertible fact', as opposed to inference and surmise, relating to the location of Roman glassmaking centres: 1. such statements of contemporary authors as could be understood and trusted; 2. references to glassmaking and glassmakers in ancient inscriptions, including the inscriptions on glass vessels; and 3. finds on the sites of ancient glass factories (Harden 1958, 48).

The first of these criteria cannot be applied to the area under consideration, since neither the Rhineland nor Britain has any Roman glassmaking centre which is referred to in classical literature, though several centres in other parts of the Roman empire are mentioned by contemporary authors (Trowbridge 1930). There is also a complete absence of epigraphic references to glass factories in these regions, except for a few glass vessels which bear initial letters on their bases; for instance, the letters C C A A which occur on a square bottle at Bonn (Fremersdorf 1965/6, 28, pl 10), and C C A which are found on two similar bottles from Silchester (Boon 1974, fig 36) and on a discoid unguent bottle from a grave at Köln-Mungersdorf (Fremersdorf 1965/6, 32, fig 4) are often taken to indicate that the vessels were made at *Colonia Claudia Ara Agrippinensis* (modern Köln). In the same way, the letters C C V which occur on a square bottle from the Bartlow Hills, Ashdon, Essex (Gage Rokewode 1842, 2-3), and on two-handled rectangular oblong bottles from Leicester and Colchester (Thorpe 1935, pl II) and at Caerleon (Boon, pers comm) may suggest that these were produced at *Colonia Claudia Victricensis* (modern Colchester). So, apart from these rather exceptional glass vessels, the only sources of 'fact' concerning individual glasshouses in the Rhineland and Britain and their products are the sites themselves and the finds which occur at these sites.

The structural remains of ancient glassmaking sites are often very difficult to identify archaeologically, and comparatively few Roman factories are known, though it is likely that many were in operation at different times in almost every part of the Roman empire.

In part, this may be explained by the nature of glassmaking, which meant that early factories were often quite small. The function of a glass furnace was only to heat the ingredients contained in one or more fireclay pots (crucibles) to a temperature sufficient to produce molten glass, as the glass was removed from the furnace in order to form the vessels. Afterwards, the finished vessels were cooled down in controlled conditions in an annealing oven which in early glasshouses was often constructed as the top storey of the furnace, above the pot chamber; this arrangement is shown on a pottery lamp of the 1st century AD from Asseria, Dalmatia (Abramić 1959, pl 27), and in a miniature in the 11th century AD manuscript of Hrabanus Maurus (eg Harden 1956, fig 309). Also, when the molten glass had been used up, production could be continued by filling up the same fireclay pots with more raw materials and heating them up again. In this way, glassmaking was a continuous process, and a great deal of glassware could be produced by a glass furnace with a very small ground-plan.

However, another important factor is the lack of characteristic waste products at most Roman glassmaking sites. Quite a lot of waste glass is created during manufacture; for instance, vessels are broken or misshapen, trails of glass spill out of the pots, and excess glass is cut away while shaping vessels or remains on the blowing iron after a vessel has been finished. Nonetheless, this scrap material is rarely found because all the broken fragments and other glass waste can be reused by melting it down in subsequent fillings of the pots, so even when a glass-working site was abandoned it generally seems to have been customary to remove the scrap glass, along with the tools and other serviceable equipment.

There is evidence for a number of Roman glassmaking sites in both the Rhineland and Britain, and in the majority of cases the most obvious surviving feature is the substructure of the furnace and other installations. For example, a series of furnace-like structures has been found at Eigelstein 35, Köln (Fremersdorf 1965/6, 39, fig 5; Doppelfeld 1966, 11, fig B), and at Wilderspool and Stockton Heath, Warrington (May 1904, 39). Other sites in Britain which have produced structural evidence for glass furnaces include Caistor-by-Norwich (Richmond 1966, fig 14) and Mancetter, Warwicks (Webster 1971, 198). Some sites have been identified because of the presence of glass which has fallen into the furnace, or of fragments of pots containing glass, as at Silchester (Boon 1974, 280), and several late Roman sites in Argonne (Chenet 1920, 256), Normandy (Dollfus 1958), and Luxembourg (Thill 1969). Many of these sites have also produced blobs of melted glass and the waste pieces removed while shaping the vessels, and a few glassmaking sites, such as the Sheepen site at Colchester (Harden 1947, 288, and pers comm), have been recognized by the presence of this material. Nearly all the glassmaking sites have produced fragments of vessel glass, and these are often taken to be the products of these factories, but this assumption should be treated with some caution since there is a great deal of evidence to suggest that the reuse of broken glass was not confined to the products of the glasshouse, and that a local trade in fragments was encouraged in suitable circumstances, so broken glass from many sources would have been collected for melting down. A system of barter, whereby broken glass vessels were exchanged for items of small worth, is recorded in operation at Rome in the later 1st century AD by Statius and Martial (Leon 1941), and it is almost certain that this or a similar system would have

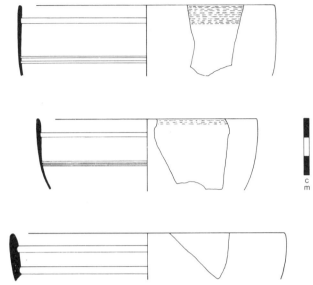

Fig 51   Fragments of three Hellenistic bowls from London

Vessel forms in Britain and the Rhineland

The second part of this paper will concentrate on some of the vessel forms in common use which occur in both the Rhineland and Britain during the Roman period, and will ignore the extremely fine luxury vessels which are found occasionally, since these are not very useful for the discussion of trade because of their great rarity.

The only reference to glass vessels imported into Britain during the Roman Empire occurs in Strabo (IV, v, 3), who was writing during the Principate of Augustus, and he states that they were imported from Gaul. In fact, there is comparatively little archaeological evidence for glass vessels at pre-conquest sites, apart from a few fragments of early Imperial cast glass which have been found at Camulodunum (Harden 1947, 288) and at other sites in south-eastern England including Silchester (Boon 1969, 34), and the cast ribbed bowl from the Welwyn-type burial at Hertford Heath (Holmes & Frend 1959, 9, pl 4), and fragments of three cast undecorated hemispherical or conical bowls found in London (Museum of London Nos 16922-4) (Fig 51), which belong to an earlier tradition of glassmaking. These late Hellenistic vessels which were produced in the eastern Mediterranean area, perhaps in the Syria-Palestine region (Weinberg 1970, 35) during the 1st century BC, are very rare in western Europe, though occasionally found at Augustan forts.

Glass-blowing had been invented nearly a century before Britain became part of the Roman Empire in AD 43, and this had caused the glass industry to change dramatically from a comparatively small-scale production apparently based at two or three centres in the eastern Mediterranean, with a limited range of forms which were expensive to produce and in many cases duplicated objects also available in pottery and metal versions, to one with factories in many Roman provinces, producing a vast range of new vessel shapes in many colours, very quickly and so, presumably, quite cheaply. Glass was never an essential substance for use in the ancient world, and its popularity depended on it being able to compete with alternative materials. However, blowing obviously made glass vessels an acceptable alternative to pottery or metal ones for the general public of the Roman world. By AD 43 most of the glass vessels being produced in the Roman Empire were blown, though several forms of cast vessels were still being produced, and the manufacture of some of these may have been stimulated by the increase in the use of glass caused by the great success of glass-blowing.

Perhaps the best known of the cast forms found at Romano-British and Rhineland sites in the first three-

been operated by glassmakers throughout the Roman Empire, at least for the production of everyday glassware. So, in many cases, the broken glass vessels found at glassmaking sites may be quite foreign to that glass factory. This being so, the information available at present which connects specific vessel forms with glass-making sites in Britain and the Rhineland is limited to the abbreviated inscriptions on the bottles already mentioned.

Despite this rather basic lack of evidence, it is sometimes possible to suggest centres or regions of manufacture for vessel forms with a limited geographical distribution on the basis of their findspots, though this can only be hypothesis and is very simplistic. Other factors affecting the distribution of these vessels, such as long-distance transport away from the place of manufacture in fulfilment of exclusive army contracts, which has been suggested for pre-Flavian fine pottery (Greene 1973, 27), cannot be taken into account. More widespread glass forms are rather difficult to interpret; they may be manufactured at one centre and traded over a wide area, or produced at several factories simultaneously, or at different dates, as a result of glassmakers moving in search of new markets and the establishment of many short-lived glasshouses to satisfy demand in different localities.

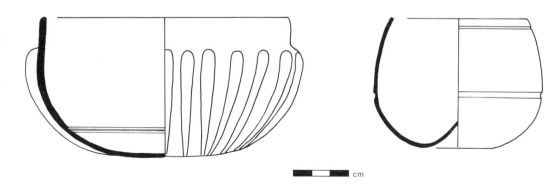

Fig 52   Pillar-moulded bowl; cast

Fig 53   'Hofheim' cup; blown

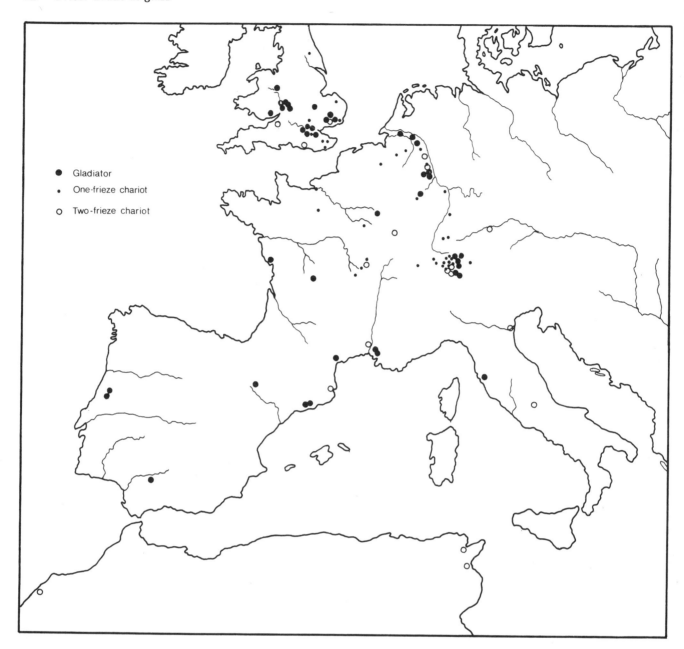

Fig 54   Distribution of cylindrical mould-blown cups with gladiatorial and chariot-racing scenes

quarters of the 1st century AD is the pillar-moulded bowl (Fig 52). Polychrome and brightly coloured specimens seem to have gone out of production in the middle of the 1st century, whereas bluish-green bowls continued in circulation, in diminishing quantities, until the end of the 1st or beginning of the 2nd century. The main centres of manufacture are not known, but since the vessels are frequently found in all parts of the Roman world it is probable that they were produced in both the eastern and the western provinces, though the locations of the factories can only be conjecture. In Italy and the western provinces centres of manufacture *may* have been established in southern, central, or northern Italy, and in southern France and/or Spain, since the bowls are extremely common in all these regions. Alternatively, they may have been widely traded from a single manufacturing centre. Most of the pillar-moulded bowls found at sites in the Rhineland and Britain exhibit a

great degree of superficial similarity; for instance, there are few obvious differences in the assemblages of these vessels at Vindonissa (Berger 1960, 15, pls 1-2), and Camulodunum (Harden 1947, 294, 298, 301, pls 87-8), and this is also true of sites established later, such as Heddernheim (Welker 1974, 18), and Fishbourne (Harden & Price 1971, 326).

The uniformity observed in the pillar-moulded bowls in these areas suggests that the same centre or centres were supplying both areas, rather than that local factories had already been set up to provide supplies in the frontier regions. This also seems to apply to the free- and mould-blown glass vessel forms found at Claudian and Neronian sites in the two areas. Most of the blown vessels found north of the Alps at this time are similar to those found in southern Switzerland, northern Italy, and southern France, and it is usually suggested that glasshouses in northern Italy, very probably at Aquileia (Calvi 1968,

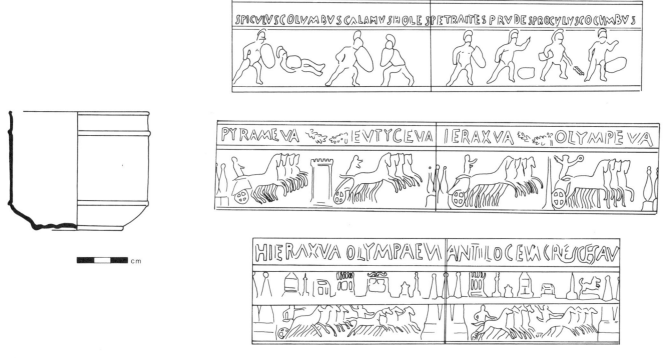

Fig 55   Profile of mould-blown cylindrical cup and main decorative friezes of gladiator, one-frieze chariot race, and two-frieze chariot race cups

passim) and in the Rhône valley, possibly at Lyons, may have been responsible for much of the production.

A drinking vessel form found quite commonly in Claudian and Neronian contexts at sites in the Rhineland and Britain and in use from the Tiberian period at Vindonissa (Berger 1960, 44) is the small blown hemispherical cup with wheel-cut lines known as the 'Hofheim' cup (Fig 53), at which site it was the most frequently recurring glass form, over 30 examples being noted by Ritterling (1913, 365). Several examples were found at Camulodunum (Harden 1947, 302), and at Fishbourne, mostly in contexts dated earlier than *c* AD 75 (Harden & Price 1971, 344). The cups seem to have gone out of production soon after AD 70 as very few examples are known from Flavian contexts; for instance, there are no fragments of the form from Heddernheim, and the evidence from Vindonissa also supports this conclusion. The cup form is a very simple blown shape, occurring at sites throughout the Roman Empire, and it is probable that it was produced at many different centres and traded locally.

Decorated mould-blown glasses also occur in Claudio-Neronian and early Flavian assemblages at sites in Britain and the Rhineland, and these have greater potential for the recognition of exact parallels than most free-blown glass. First century mould-blown glass vessels with inscriptions stating the name of the maker (Harden 1935), are very rare at sites north of the Alps, though signed negro-head beakers are known from Caerleon and London (Price 1974), but the products of a single mould can sometimes be recognized. Although the geographical location of the factories producing mould-blown vessels cannot be established beyond doubt until fragments of the moulds are found at glassmaking sites, the distribution of identical vessels may be a useful indicator as to the approximate whereabouts of such factories.

Three groups of early mould-blown glass occur in the Rhineland and Britain. First, there are a very few vessels which were almost certainly made by eastern glassmakers and transported to the northern and western provinces, or perhaps were made at branch factories set up somewhere in north-eastern Italy. The second group consists of vessels such as almond-knobbed beakers and hemispherical ribbed bowls which are found on sites throughout the Roman Empire at about the same time, and which were probably made at a number of centres. Both forms are represented at Vindonissa (Berger 1960, 52), and occur at other Rhineland sites. The volume of trade into Britain was not large, and like the first group, these vessels may only represent personal possessions brought into Britain, perhaps by military personnel, since many of the pieces have been found in Neronian or early Flavian contexts at military sites. The third group consists of cylindrical cups and ovoid beakers showing circus scenes, and the distribution of these vessels is confined to the western parts of the Roman Empire, with the vast majority of finds occurring in the north-western provinces.

The distribution of cylindrical cups depicting gladiatorial contests and scenes of chariot-racing is shown in Fig 54, and the form of the cup and the principal design friezes are illustrated in Fig 55. These cups are concentrated in the Rhineland, mostly at military stations and especially at Vindonissa (Berger 1960, 56), and in Britain where many of the pieces also come from military sites. In general, the gladiator and one-frieze chariot cups have rather similar distributions, with the exception of Iberia, where the designs on many of the gladiator cups are quite different from those found in other provinces (Price 1975, 69). The two-frieze chariot cups are more widely spread and are the only type known to occur at North African sites. They are also the most varied in their design elements, and mould parallels are rare, except for the Ham Hill/Tunis/Orange group and the Camulo-

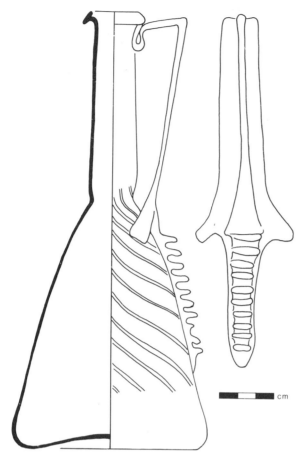

Fig 56   Conical jug with angular handle

dunum/Neuss/Vindonissa group (Harden & Price 1971, 337). By contrast, the gladiator and one-frieze chariot cups are more uniform. About 50 cylindrical gladiator cups are known, and only a few have combat scenes or named gladiators which differ markedly from those shown in Fig 55. The one-frieze chariot cups also have a standardized format, with only a little variation in the designs of the four quadrigae and the names of the charioteers.

Many of the cups found at Rhineland and Romano-British sites come from Neronian or early Flavian contexts, and the archaeological evidence is supported by literary sources which suggest that the gladiator cups at least were produced during the reign of Nero (Rowell 1958). Many years ago, Harden (1940, 104) suggested that these mould-blown circus cups were made at a centre in the Rhône valley, perhaps at Lyons, or Marseilles, or in the Allier region. Although the distribution of these cups does not obviously support this view, it is interesting that fragments of terracotta moulds, perhaps part of a body-mould for one-frieze chariot cups, were found quite recently at Mariana in Corsica, though not from a glass-making site (Mme G Morrachini-Mazel, pers comm). Some form of trade to the northern and western frontier provinces from the manufacturing centre is certainly indicated, rather than these cups merely being carried about as the personal possessions of military personnel who knew and cared about the sporting heroes of the day in Rome, because otherwise it is almost certain that some of these vessels would have been found in other provinces of the Empire, such as the lower Danube region and the eastern frontiers.

The first vessel forms which are not also found at sites south of the Alps appear in the late Neronian/early Flavian period and it is very probable that these were made at glasshouses in central or northern France, or the Rhineland. Although there is archaeological evidence for a glasshouse at Köln by AD 50 (Fremersdorf 1965/6; Doppelfeld 1966, 10) it is not easy to identify the early vessels made at this centre, or to be certain that this was the only glassmaking centre functioning in the north-western provinces at this time. The vessels under discussion are long-necked conical or globular bodied jugs with angular handles ending in a claw attachment on the upper body, and often with a pinched trail extending down the body from the middle of the handle (Fig 56), and globular jars with a folded tubular rim formed into a collar (Fig 57), and they are found at sites in Britain, central and northern France, Belgium and Holland, and the lower and middle Rhineland in later 1st and early 2nd century contexts (Isings 1957, 70, 88). The limits of distribution are not exactly defined, but there are no fragments of these vessels at Vindonissa, though the jug form occurs at Hofheim, and fragmentary examples of both are known at Heddernheim. In France, jars have been found at Besançon (Morin-Jean 1913, fig 55), and at Clermont-Ferrand, but neither form is known in the museums of the Rhône valley south of Lyons. Some of the jugs bear an applied 'Medusa head' medallion, often at the base of the handle (eg Fox 1923, pl 25,4), and these have a certain amount of potential for the recognition of products of glassmaking sites in the lower Rhineland and northern France through the identification of medallions made by the same stamps, as each of the stamps was presumably used by one or more glassmakers working from the same glasshouse.

From the Flavian period onwards there is less dependence on the products of glasshouses in other areas, and the glass assemblages of the Rhineland, northern France, and Britain develop characteristics which distinguish them from contemporary material found elsewhere in the empire. However, some contact between glassmaking centres seems to continue, and the glass industry of the Rhineland and northern provinces never becomes totally detached from external influences. The 'snake-thread' glass of the 2nd and 3rd centuries is a clear example of contact between the eastern and

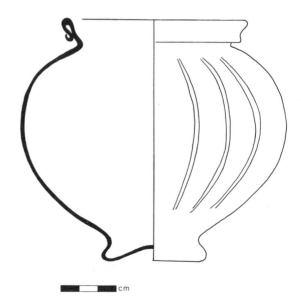

Fig 57   Globular jar with collar rim

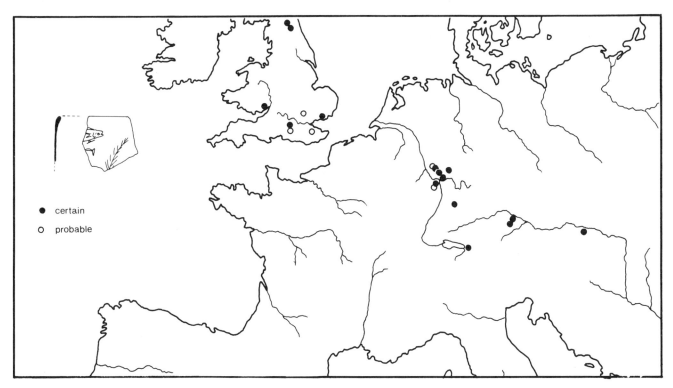

certain ●
probable ○

Fig 58 Distribution of fragmentary cylindrical cups with engraved fishes and inscriptions (after Charlesworth 1959, with additions)

Rhineland glasshouses, as production of this glass seems to have begun in the eastern Mediterranean area (Harden 1934) before it was made in the western provinces, although far more is known in the west. It is easy to accept that Köln was a major producer of this glass, in view of the large numbers of fine pieces which have been found in burials in the city and the surrounding region (Fremersdorf 1959, passim), and it is also possible that similar vessels were made in Belgium or northern France. This very distinctively decorated glass was extremely common in the Rhineland, northern France, Belgium, and Holland, and also seems to have been traded over considerable distances, as fragments are known from sites in northern Spain and Italy. However, comparatively little has been found on Romano-British sites, and it is not possible to explain this phenomenon satisfactorily, though it might be conjectured that other regions were absorbing most of the production, or that there was no market in Britain for this type of glass, either because it was not competitive with the local alternatives or because the consumers did not like the glass!

By contrast, the colourless cylindrical cups which are also thought to be the products of Rhineland glasshouses in the 2nd and 3rd centuries (Fremersdorf 1970) are very common indeed at many sites in Britain, as at Corbridge, where 30-40 examples have been recorded (Bulmer 1955, 128). These cups are usually undecorated, but painted examples are also known (Fremersdorf 1970) and there is a small group of fragmentary cups engraved with fishes and inscriptions, with palm fronds as stops (see Fig 58). Most of these have been found in the forts and their extra-mural civilian settlements on the Danube, Rhine, and northern British frontiers in later 2nd and early 3rd century contexts. Too few of the fragmentary cups survive for definite conclusions to be drawn from this distribution, but Köln does not stand out clearly as the

centre for manufacture of these decorated cups, though it should be borne in mind that the vessels need not have been decorated in the same place as they were made, since the two processes are quite independent and were carried out by different groups of craftsmen.

A wide variety of cut and engraved glass vessels occurs in late 3rd and 4th century contexts at Rhineland sites, and most of the types are represented by fragments on Romano-British sites; a clearly defined group of bowls bearing mythological, biblical, or hunting scenes engraved free-hand with a flint burin, which occurs at sites in the Rhineland, northern France, and Britain, with one bowl travelling as far as Altafulla in north-eastern Spain, has been identified by Harden (1960) as the product of one factory operating at Köln in the 4th century (see Fig 59), and other schools of cutting were probably also centred in the lower Rhineland.

There was considerable change in the everyday glass wares of the north-western provinces during the 4th century; much of it was made of greenish-yellow glass, instead of the bluish-green which had been common in the 1st to 3rd centuries AD, and there was a great deal of local variation in vessel forms, probably indicating that many small glasshouses were at work, instead of a few larger ones. Roman Britain did not lose contact with the continental glasshouses, but the very late imported common glass vessels can perhaps be related more closely to finds from northern France and Belgium and Holland than to contemporary material from Rhineland sites, though there was always a great deal of overlap of the forms in use.

Containers

Several different forms of glass vessels, such as square and cylindrical bottles, square jars, and unguentaria, were produced during the Roman period in order to

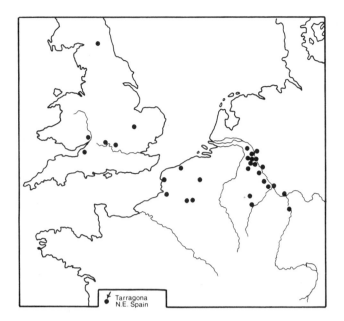

Fig 59　Distribution of 4th century AD bowls with engraved hunting, biblical, and mythological scenes (after Harden 1960, with additions)

contain liquid or semi-liquid substances, and these vessels were moved from place to place and bought and sold because of their contents, not as objects of trade in their own right. Many of the vessels have designs on their bases, and the study of the distribution of vessels with similar basal designs can be very useful for recognizing areas supplied by different producers, though in most cases it is not yet clear whether the designs on the bottle bases relate to the bottle makers or to the concern for whom the bottles were made. Square bottles are probably the commonest of the Roman glass containers, and they occur in very large numbers in 1st and 2nd century contexts throughout the Roman world, though more of them are known in Italy and the western provinces than further to the east (Isings 1957, 63;

Charlesworth 1966). There are many different forms of basal design, ranging from a series of concentric circles to scenes showing (?) beavers eating (?) cherries, and inscriptions giving proper names, and all but the simplest of these designs show regional variation; in this matter, it is interesting to compare some of the bottle stamps found on Romano-British sites (Charlesworth 1959, fig 9) with those from Roman Portugal (Alarcão 1976). The bottle stamps from Britain are very similar to those from sites in northern France and the Rhineland, but most of these groups have only very few surviving examples (see Fig 60). The vessels shown on this map have a base stamp which reads AF, or AF enclosed by a Q, and several moulds were clearly used to produce the bottles; it has recently been suggested (Welker 1974, 74) that these bottles might have been made in Britain, but too few specimens are known to establish the centre of manufacture with any certainty. The discovery of the patterned moulds into which the vessels were blown would be of very great assistance for establishing the centres of manufacture, but these have not yet been recognized at sites in Britain or the Rhineland, except for the terracotta fragment found at Köln in 1927 with the negative impression of four concentric circles and angle pieces at three surviving corners, which has been claimed as a square bottle base mould (Fremersdorf 1965/6, 32, fig 2.9).

Square bottles went out of production in the later 2nd or early 3rd century AD, and no other glass vessel form seems to have taken their place, though a group of mould-blown cylindrical or barrel-shaped bottles, often called 'Frontinus bottles' because of the abbreviated name found on the bases of many of them, must have served the same purpose in the north-western part of the Roman Empire in the 3rd and 4th centuries AD (Isings 1957, 106). These vessels occur in large numbers in northern France where they were probably made, and are widely distributed in the Rhineland, but only a very few have been recognized at Romano-British sites (Fig 61).

Throughout the Roman period, the volume of trade in glass into Britain appears to have been very slight, and in

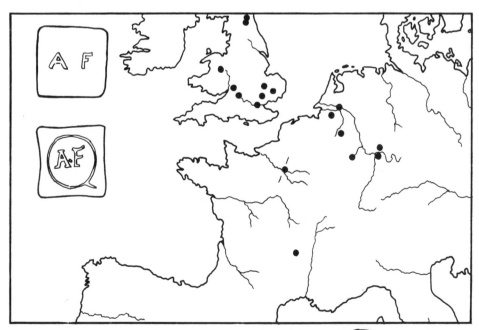

Fig 60　Distribution of square bottles with AF and ⟨AF⟩ stamps

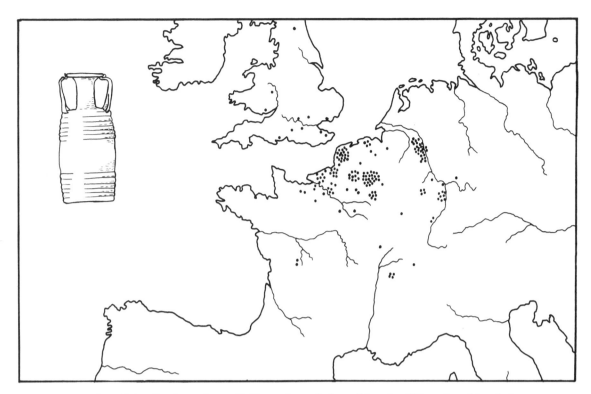

Fig 61   Distribution of mould-blown barrel-shaped bottles ('Frontinus' bottles)

many instances the vessels surviving might have arrived in a single packing case. However, this impression may be very misleading indeed as the survival of glass vessels is very much a matter of chance; unless the glass vessels were used as grave goods in burials, which is perhaps less usual in Britain than in the Rhineland, or were thrown away during the abandonment of a site, they were very likely to have been melted down soon after breakage to make new vessels or window glass or beads, in which case the trade of glass into Britain and the amount of glass produced by the Romano-British glasshouses may have been very much larger than the surviving fragments suggest. It is probable that glass was always a rarer commodity in Britain than in the Rhineland, and that much of the fine tableware on Romano-British sites was imported from that region, since vessel glass was manufactured on a large scale in the lower Rhineland, especially at Köln, from the middle of the 1st century AD onwards.

This essay is not intended to be a comprehensive survey of the trade in glass vessels between Britain and the Rhineland in the Roman period, but has examined the archaeological evidence for a few forms which occur in both areas, using them to illustrate different aspects of distribution and to suggest various commercial operations. However, since so little is known at present about the Roman glass industry in these regions there is not much chance of a satisfactory interpretation of these trading patterns.

References

Abramić, M, 1959   Eine römische Lampe mit Darstellung des Glasblasens, *Bonner Jahrbücher*, **159**, 149-51.

Alarcão, J, 1976   Bouteilles carrées à fond décoré du Portugal romain, *J Glass Stud*, **17**, 47-53.

Berger, L, 1960   *Römische Gläser aus Vindonissa*.

Boon, G C, 1969   Belgic and Roman Silchester: the excavations of 1954-8 with an excursus on the early history of Calleva, *Archaeologia*, **102**, 1-81.

——, 1974   *Silchester; the Roman town of Calleva*.

Bulmer, W, 1955   Roman glass vessels in the Corstopitum museum, Corbridge, *Archaeol Aeliana*, 4 ser, **33**, 116-33.

Calvi, M C, 1968   *I Vetri Romani del Museo di Aquileia*.

Charlesworth, D, 1959   Roman glass in Northern Britain, *Archaeol Aeliana*, 4 ser, **37**, 33-58.

——, 1966   Roman square bottles, *J Glass Stud*, **8**, 26-40.

Chenet, G, 1920   Anciennes Verreries d'Argonne, *Bulletin Archéologique*.

Dollfus, M-A, 1958   Les poteries à couverte de verre (creuset de verriers?) d'époque Gallo-Romaine découvertes à Lyons-le-Forêt (Eure), *Revue des Societés Savants de la Haute Normandie*, **10**, 37-41.

Doppelfeld, O, 1966   *Römisches und fränkisches Glas in Köln*.

Fox, C, 1923   *The archaeology of the Cambridge region*.

Fremersdorf, F, 1959   *Römische Gläser mit Fadenauflage in Köln*.

——, 1965/6   Die Anfange der römischen Glashütten Kölns, *Kölner Jahrbücher*, **8**, 24-43.

——, 1970   Seltene Varianten steilwandiger römischer Glasbecher des 3Jh aus Köln, *ibid*, **11**, 59-72.

Gage Rokewode, J, 1842   Account of the final excavations made at the Bartlow Hills, *Archaeologia*, **29**, 1-4.

Greene, K, 1973   The pottery from Usk, in *Current research in Romano-British coarse pottery* (ed A Detsicas), CBA Res Rep **10**, 25-37.

Harden, D B, 1934   Snake-thread glasses found in the East, *J Roman Stud*, **24**, 50-5.

——, 1935   Romano-Syrian glasses with mould-blown inscriptions, *ibid*, **25**, 163-86.

——, 1940   Roman mould blown glasses, *The Connoisseur*, **106**, 102-5.

——, 1947   The glass, in *Camulodunum* (C F C Hawkes & M R Hull), 287-307.

——, 1956   Glass and glazes, in *A history of technology* II (C Singer et al), 311-46.

——, 1958   Glassmaking centres and the spread of glass-making from the first to the fourth century AD, *Annales du 1er Congrès des 'Journées Internationales du Verre'*, 47-62.

——, 1960   The Wint Hill hunting bowl and related glasses, *J Glass Studies*, **2**, 44-81.

Harden, D B, & Price, J, 1971   The glass, in *Excavations at Fishbourne 1961-1969* (B W Cunliffe), 317-68.f

Holmes, J, & Frend, W H C, 1959   A Belgic chieftain's grave on Hertford Heath, *E Herts Archaeol Soc Trans*, **14**, 1-19.

Isings, C, 1957   *Roman glass from dated finds.*

Jones, H L, 1923   *The Geography of Strabo, II* (Loeb Classical Library).

Leon, H J, 1941   Sulphur for broken glass, *Trans Proc American Philological Ass,* **72,** 233-6.

May, T, 1904   *Warrington's Roman remains.*

Morin-Jean, 1913   *La Verrerie en Gaule sous l'Empire Romain.*

Price, J, 1974   A Roman mould-blown Negro-head glass beaker from London, *Antiq J,* **54,** 291-2.

——, 1975   Some Roman glass from Spain, *Annales de 6ᵉ Congrès de l'Association Internationale pour l'Histoire du Verre,* 65-84.

Richmond, I A, 1966   Industry in Roman Britain, in *The civitas capitals of Roman Britain* (ed J S Wacher), 76-86.

Ritterling, E, 1913   *Das frührömische Lager bei Hofheim im Taunus,* Annalen des Vereins für Nassauische Altertumskunde und Geschichtsforschung, **40.**

Rowell, H T, 1958   The Gladiator Petraites and the date of the *Satyricon, Trans Proc American Philological Ass,* **89,** 14-24.

Thill, G, 1969   Une verrerie gallo-romaine au Titelberg, *Hémecht,* 521-8.

Thorpe, W A, 1935   *English glass.*

Trowbridge, M L, 1930   *Philological studies in ancient glass,* Univ Illinois Studies in Language and Literature, **13,** 3-4.

Webster, G, 1971   Roman Warwickshire, *Archaeol J,* **128,** 196-9.

Weinberg, G D, 1970   Hellenistic glass from Tel Anafa in Upper Galilee, *J Glass Stud,* **12,** 17-27.

——, 1973   Notes on glass from Upper Galilee, *ibid,* **15,** 35-51.

Welker, E, 1974   *Die römischen Gläser von Nida-Heddernheim.*

John Peter Wild

There is no contemporary handbook on cross-channel trade in the Roman period to match that of the nameless shipper or skipper of the *Periplus of the Erythraean Sea*—and he could hardly be further removed from the Channel, for his interests lay in the trading connections with the Arab states and India.[1] Without a *periplus,* we must learn about Channel trade the hard way.

From the first the conference revealed a dichotomy of interest between those concerned with the ships and those concerned with the cargoes carried in them. This was to be expected. But as discussion proceeded many potential points of contact between the two spheres of interest dropped away. As Mark Hassall aptly commented from the chair: 'We have seen the ships that did *not* cross the Channel; now we learn of the goods that were *not* carried in them'.

In this discussion I shall examine some aspects of the textile trade and the questions of wider interest which they raise for the conference. I shall survey the textile fabrics as objects of trade, the merchants who carried them, and the mechanics of transporting textiles.

The textile fabrics

Imports

The late Professor A H M Jones (1960) held the view that household weaving was of little economic importance. Even the poorest bought ready-made clothing[2] and weaving was in the main a professional occupation. This may perhaps have been true of Italy and some other Mediterranean provinces, but the extant textiles from the north-west suggest that Jones's thesis oversimplifies the situation, and underestimates the role of domestic weavers.

A number of textiles found in Roman Britain can plausibly be claimed as imports. A secondary burial in the Roman barrow at Holborough, Snodland, Kent, contained small fragments of damask silk, woven perhaps in a Syrian workshop in the 3rd century AD (Wild 1965, 246ff). A small piece of plain-weave silk was noted amongst the contents of the Roman sewer at York (MacGregor 1976, 14f), and this, too, may be an eastern Mediterranean product. Silk-weavers may have been at work in the Latin-speaking west (Wild 1970, 51), but there is no sign of their presence in Britain—and their raw materials would certainly have been imported.

There are a number of finds of textiles in Britain embroidered or interwoven with gold thread. The 'thread' consists of a fine ribbon of gold wound spirally around a textile fibre core, usually of silk. The occupant of the late Iron-Age *Fürstengrab* at Lexden near Colchester was able to obtain from the Continent cloth of gold, presumably through the same channels as he obtained the other luxury goods of Roman origin in his tomb. Gold thread of Roman date is attested on Romano-British sites, eg in a late Roman grave at Poundbury, Dorset (unpublished, but see *Britannia* 1 (1970), 299; cf Wild 1970, 131, table H), but more striking is the amount and richness of Anglo-Saxon cloth carrying gold thread (Crowfoot & Hawkes 1967; *Medieval Archaeol,* 13 (1969), 209f). Golden textiles of this type were evidently popular from a very early date

and were imported at every period, regardless of the fluctuations in cross-channel communication.

Exotic textiles are easy enough to recognize as imports. But in the middle ranges of the market—in woollens as in glassware (pp 70-8)—the criteria for establishing origins are more subjective. In broad terms the spin-direction of the yarns can give a clue to source, but it does not enable us to attribute textiles to a specific province (Wild 1970, 44f).

Woollen cloth-fragments from Vindolanda-Chesterholm (Wild, in press) and from the Walbrook in London (Wild 1975) illustrates the difficulty. They carry tapestry-woven bands as decoration, a technique not familiar to the Iron Age weaver or her immediate successors in Roman Britain. Although tapestry weaving was most at home in the eastern Mediterranean (Wild 1967), it is quite possible for the tapestry weavers to have followed their market, like the Arretine and samian potters, and to have set up their looms as immigrant craftsmen in Britain. I suspect, however, that the Vindolanda piece may have been imported, but I admit that this is hardly more than a guess.

The source of linen is equally difficult to prove. The later Roman burials at York, for example, show that high-quality household linen was quite commonplace in the *colonia* (RCHM 1962, 108f). Direct evidence, however, for flax growing and linen manufacture in Roman Britain is minimal.[3] But this is no argument in itself for a linen trade.

The total sum of proven textile imports into Britain is so small (less than 2% of the extant textiles) that one must face the question raised by other contributors: did the material arrive on a foreign traveller's back or in his luggage? If so, it does not provide evidence of trade. A single thread of cotton from a well at Chew Stoke, for instance, does not attest regular importation of cotton cloth into Britain (Biek 1963, 148; Rahtz 1978). Rather, it is a parallel to the finds of cotton, silk, and *pinna* in the graves of Syrian or Egyptian immigrants at Budapest, who presumably brought the fabrics north as personal possessions (Nagy 1935, 3ff; Póczy 1964; 1966). Nevertheless, I submit that at least the silks mentioned above point to regular commerce in that commodity; it is no coincidence that the term for silk in Old Welsh is a loanword borrowed through the medium of Roman Britain (Jackson 1953, 78).

Exports

While the evidence for textile imports set out above is largely archaeological, the evidence for British exports depends on written sources. The Edict of Diocletian (AD 301) provides a comprehensive (but not quite complete) list of the main consumer goods bought and sold within the Roman Empire, together with their maximum permitted prices (Lauffer 1971; Giacchero 1974). In Chapter XIX,48 British woollen capes (*byrri*) are of medium quality, to judge by their price level, but in XIX, 28-9 British rugs (*tapetia*), which come in two qualities, are at the head of their class—a great achievement, if one considers the centuries, if not millennia, of rug-making experience in the eastern provinces (Wace 1972). Textiles are the only British products to be listed in the Edict, and these entries, taken at face value, imply that the woollen industry was economically the leading British enterprise. Surviving textiles tend to bear this out.

So far as the Edict is concerned, cross-channel textile trade was in finished or semi-finished articles, to which minor modifications might have to be made by the purchaser.[4] British raw wool is not attested as a separate commodity. This may seem odd to students of the English wool trade in the early Middle Ages, but in the Edict the section on raw wool (XXV, 1-13) is quite short. The terracotta model of a bale of green-dyed wool found in the broch of Dun an Iardhard on Skye may imply that there was some traffic in dyed wool, but it is far from certain (Curle 1931-2, 289-90, fig 2; Richmond 1958, 26f). We should not forget that in AD 796, when Charlemagne sought from Offa the revitalization of the English wool trade, he was concerned with finished garments, not bales of wool (Wallace-Hadrill 1966, 693).

The merchants

The epigraphic sources contain no explicit reference to *negotiatores* engaged in the textile trade between Britain and the Rhineland. The group of inscriptions from Domburg and Colijnsplaat at the Rhine mouth, discussed by Mark Hassall (pp 41-8), is potentially the most fruitful source of such information. The *absence* of *negotiatores vestiarii* or *sagarii* there may be thought significant. On the other hand we cannot be sure that the circle of devotees of Nehalennia was a genuine cross-section of commercial society on the Lower Rhine. A special plea might be made for Placidus, the *negotiator Britannicianus* from Colijnsplaat, for his tribe, the Veliocasses, had some connection with flax growing and linen may have been among his wares.[5]

A tombstone from Stockum near Düsseldorf (*CIL*. XIII. 8568; Weisgerber 1968, 134ff) commemorates L Priminius Ingenuus, a *negotiator vestiarius importator*. His name is of Rhenish origin and it would have passed unremarked among the Rhinelanders at Domburg or Colijnsplaat. His main business was probably the sale of textiles to the garrison of the fort at Neuss and nearby military sites along the Rhine (von Petrikovits 1960, 124). He may well have received his goods by sea and river from Britain—or perhaps from the wool-producing areas of Gallia Belgica.

Mark Hassall has made the attractive suggestion that Fufidius, the *negotiator* 'from the province of Britain', who was buried at Mainz-Kastel, was a *negotiator vestiarius*.[6] If this is so, then the Mainz garrison must have been his best customers, and some of the textiles found in Mainz may have been his wares (Wild 1970, 42). Another merchant with a base in Upper Germany was Maxsiminus, who paid a vow to Mercury at Marsal, a small town just over the border in Gallia Belgica (*CIL*. XIII. 4564). He, too, was a *negotiator vestiarius*, and in that region was much more likely to be an importer of clothing than an exporter.

The commercial travellers whom we have considered above pale into insignificance when they are compared with the wealthy freedmen engaged in the textile trade and in textile manufacture in southern Gaul (*CIL*. XIII. 2010, 2003; XII. 4422, 1898; XIII. 542, 1998). M Messius Fortunatus, freedman and *sevir Augustalis*, who records his presence in AD 225 at Rottenburg on the Neckar in Upper Germany (*CIL*. XIII. 6366), is more in the southern mould. He describes himself as a dealer in pottery and military capes. In general the northern

textile trade may simply not have been of sufficient volume to attract such entrepreneurs.

Textile merchants in northern Gaul—whether selling cloaks (*saga*), capes (*paenulae*), or general textiles (*vestimenta*)—dealt in woollen goods. No direct evidence for a linen trade has yet been found. This fits well with the picture given by the Edict of Diocletian.

An important general point arising from this and from earlier discussions is that the presence of the army was a stimulus to trade. This can be clearly demonstrated in the case of the Gallic pottery industry, where both the products and the potters followed the military markets. The role of the army in the romanization of the frontier provinces has long been recognized; its contribution to the creation of a viable economic structure in the north-western provinces would be hard to overestimate. The army was obliged to supply its soldiers at least with the basic clothing they required, and bulk orders placed by the general stores would be attractive to *negotiatores* (Wild 1976). However, wherever possible, clothing was bought locally, often with an element of compulsory purchase. The collection of woollen cloth from the pre-Hadrianic fort at Vindolanda lends archaeological support to this view, for the homogeneity of the weaves and the character of the wool fibres strongly suggest local production. Few textiles would have arrived at the fort through the hands of *negotiatores vestiarii*, but fond relations sometimes sent a clothing parcel to their sons or nephews (Wild, in press).

Transport of textiles

Textiles have an advantage over many other types of cargo in that they are easy to make up into bales of a convenient size and are not readily damaged or spoilt in transit. Transfer from wagon to ship or from river-barge to seagoing vessel presents few problems.

The scenes on the grave monument of the Secundinii at Igel near Trier (Dragendorff & Kruger 1924) illustrate my point. Individual panels show the peasants on a great estate delivering the cloth which they have woven to the landowner's warehouse (op cit Taf 10.1), servants roping up huge bales of cloth (op cit 56, Abb 33), and a barge carrying two bales being towed along the Moselle or Saar (op cit Taf 16,3; cf Espérandieu 1907-38, nos 4120, 5261).

The most expensive textiles travelled immense distances between their production centres and the ultimate purchaser. Silk fabrics of Chinese origin have been found at Palmyra in Syria (Pfister 1937, 35-8; Pfister & Bellinger 1945, 3) and silk damask woven in Syria from imported Chinese silk has been found in the north-west provinces (Wild 1970, 50ff). In times of economic dislocation the volume of textile trade dwindled, but high-quality wool cloth and silk was still found to be worth the cost, risk, and effort of transporting (Hundt 1969; Crowfoot & Hawkes 1967; Böhner 1958).

We still know very little about the *modus operandi* of the northern *negotiatores*. Comparative costs of land and sea transport suggest that they would have preferred the latter, wherever practical, since it was substantially cheaper (Duncan-Jones 1974, 368). Dr Peacock has already shown how transport costs may have affected the distribution of wine carried in the amphorae of Dressel form 30 (pp 49-51). Two constitutions in the Theodosian Code (ed Mommsen 1905: VIII. 5,47 and VIII. 5,48— AD 386) reveal that express wagons of the imperial post (*raedae*) had an optimum capacity of 1000 lb weight of linen; if the consignment was heavier, it had to go by boat!

The *negotiatores vestiarii* may have owned their own ships, or alternatively they may have entrusted the transport of their goods to a *nauta* or shipper like Blussus at Mainz (*CIL*. XIII. 7067) or Vegisonius Martinus at Colijnsplaat. This at least would have solved the problem of returning with a vessel in ballast, for the *nauta*, like a haulage contractor, could take a return load of another commodity.

The conference, it seems to me, has made progress on two fronts. Firstly, the state of research in a series of interconnected fields had been put on record. None of the contributors can now claim to be working in isolation! Secondly, attention has been drawn to a number of problems which prevent us at present from turning the archaeological and related evidence into technological or economic history.

As I see it, the crucial questions are:

a Have we yet seen any of the ships which regularly carried cross-channel cargoes?

b How can we recognize in the archaeological record the difference between imported personal possessions and imported commercial goods?

c Who owned the ships and how was the trade organized?

d What was the place of the military market in the wider economic context?

A problem shared may one day be a problem solved.

Notes

1 *The Periplus of the Erythraean Sea* (ed W H Schoff, 1912); *Le Périple de la Mer Erythreé* (ed H Frisk, 1927); for its date see J I Miller, *The spice trade of the Roman Empire 29 BC-AD 641*, Oxford 1969, 16ff (AD 85); *Numismatic Chronicle,* **10,** 1970, 221ff (*c* AD 100).

2 See *Edictum Diocletiani* (ed S Lauffer, 1971) XXVI, *passim*.

3 Wild 1970, 15. Some flax was grown in Yorkshire in the 19th century: *The Victoria History of the Counties of England, Yorkshire* II, London 1912, 479.

4 The tailor's services listed in the Edict (VII, 42-63) make more sense in connection with clothing bought on the open market than with clothing woven in the home, where the housewife herself would surely put the finishing touches to it.

5 *Deae Nehalenniae: Gids bij de tentoonstelling Nehalennia de zeeuwse godin*, Middelburg-Leiden 1971, no 45; Veliocasses: *CIL*. XIII. 1998; for flax in that region: Pliny, *NH* XIX, 8. M Verec(undius) Diogenes, *sevir* of the *colonia* of York (*RIB*. 678. 687) and probably a merchant (*J Roman Stud,* **56,** 1966, 228) also originated in a flax-growing area.

6 *CIL*. XIII. 7300. [VESTI]ARIO is a possible reconstruction; but there is room for six letters in the gap.

References

Biek, L, 1963   *Archaeology and the microscope.*
Böhner, K, 1958   Das Grab eines fränkischen Herrn aus Morken im Rheinland, *Neue Ausgrabungen in Deutschland*, 432ff.
Crowfoot, E, & Hawkes, S Chadwick, 1967   Early Anglo-Saxon gold braids, *Medieval Archaeol,* **11,** 42-86.
Curle, J, 1931-2   An inventory of objects of Roman and provincial Roman origin found on sites in Scotland, *Proc Soc Antiq Scot,* **66,** 277ff.
Dragendorff, H, & Krüger, E, 1924   *Das Grabmal von Igel.*
Duncan-Jones, R, 1974   *The economy of the Roman Empire.*

Espérandieu, E, 1907-38   *Receuil général des bas-reliefs, statues et bustes de la Gaule Romaine.*
Giacchero, M, 1974   *Edictum Diocletiani, Pubbl dell'Instituto di Storia Antica e Scienze Ausiliare dell'Università di Genova,* **8.**
Hundt, H-J, 1969   Über vorgeschichtliche Seidenfunde, *Jahrbuch des römisch-germanischen Zentralmuseum,* **16,** 59-71.
Jackson, K H, 1953   *Language and history in early Britain.*
Jones, A H M, 1960   The cloth industry under the Roman Empire, *Econ Hist Rev*, n ser, **13,** 184ff (reprinted in *The Roman economy: studies in ancient economic and administrative history* (A H M Jones, ed P A Brunt), Oxford 1974, 351ff).
Lauffer, S, 1971   *Diokletians Preisedikt.*
MacGregor, A, 1976   *Finds from a Roman sewer system and an adjacent building in Church Street, The archaeology of York,* 17/1.
Nagy, L, 1935   *Aquincumi Múmia-Temetkezések, Dissertationes Pannonicae,* **1,** 4.
Petrikovits, H von, 1960   *Das römische Rheinland: archäologische Forschungen seit 1945.*
Pfister, R, 1937   *Nouveaux textiles de Palmyre.*
Pfister, R, & Bellinger, L, 1945   *The excavations at Dura-Europos, Final report,* **4,** 2, *The textiles.*
Póczy, K S, 1964   Ujabb aquincumi múmiasír, *Archaeologiai Ertesítö,* **91,** 176ff.
——, 1966   Festett férfiportré egy aquincumi múmia-sírból, *ibid,* **93,** 272-7.
RCHM 1962   *An inventory of the historical monuments in the city of York,* I, *Eburacum: Roman York*, Royal Commission on Historical Monuments (England).
Rahtz, P A, 1978   *Excavations at Chew Valley Lake, Somerset,* HMSO.
Richmond, I A (ed), 1958   *Roman and native in North Britain.*
Wace, A J B, 1972   Tappeto, *American J Archaeol,* **76,** 438-40.
Wallace-Hadrill, J M, 1966   Charlemagne and England, in *Karl der Grosse: Lebenswerk und Nachleben* I (ed W Braunfels).
Weisgerber, L, 1968   *Die Namen der Ubier.*
Wild, J P, 1965   A Roman silk damask from Kent, *Archaeol Cantiana,* **80,** 246-50.
——, 1967   Two technical terms used by Roman tapestry-weavers, *Philologus,* **3,** 151-5.
——, 1970   *Textile manufacture in the northern Roman provinces.*
——, 1975   Roman textiles from the Walbrook (London), *Germania,* **53,** 138-43.
——, 1976   The gynaecea, in *Aspects of the Notitia Dignitatum* (eds R G Goodburn & O Bartholomew), BAR supp ser **15,** 51ff.
——, in press   *The textiles from Vindolanda 1973-1975.*

Index

Abbeville, France, 20
actores navium, 46
alae, Germanic in Britain, 41
Alet, Brittany, 59
Algeria, Dressel 30 manufacture, 50
Alice Holt Forest (Surrey) kilns, 60, 64
allecarii, 44
Altafulla, Spain, 75
altars, set up by traders etc, 41, 43, 44, 58
amphorae, for African oil, 59, 63; Bi, Bii, and Biv types, 49, 63; in
    Britain, 49-51; Dressel 1, 50; Dr 20, 51; Dr 30, 49-51; on mosaic, 35;
    North African cylindrical, 50; transport of, 13
anchor stones, 30
Aquileia, Italy, 56, 72
Aquitaine, 51
Argonne, France, glass from, 70
Arisenius Marius (lib), 43 (Tab I)
Arles, France, mint, 59, 65
Arlon, Belgium, 51
Arrezzo, Italy, 56
Asprius A [. . . , 43 (Tab II)
Asseria, Dalmatia, 70
Aurelius C L Verus, C, 43 (Tab II)
Aurelius Lunaris, M, 42, 43 (Tab II), 46, 51
Austruweel, Antwerp, Netherlands, 3
Avenches, Switzerland, Roman port, 31

Bad Kreuznach, Rheinland-Pfalz, ship-mosaic, 1, 11, 35
barges, typology, 20; Bevaix, 15, 20, 25, 31, 32, 33-5; Druten, 16, 20,
    25; ferry-type, 15; heavy barges, see *Oberländer*; Kapel Avezaath,
    16, 20, 31; Pommeroeul, 22-3; Utrecht type, 20; Vechten boat, 16;
    Yverdon, 15, 20, 25, 31, 32, 35; Zwammerdam, 15-21, 25;
    Zwammerdam nos 2, 4, and 6, 16-17, 18 (fig 21), 19 (figs 22-3), 31
barrels, 13, 45, 51, 67
Bartlow Hills, Ashdon, Essex, 70
Batavians, 41
Bath, visitors from Moselle, 42
Baynard's Castle, London, 38
Beckfoot, Cumbria, 36, 37
Belisarius, invasion fleet of, 67
Besançon, France, 74
Bevaix, Switzerland, boat, 15, 20, 25, 31-5; caulking, 32
bilge strakes, L-shaped, 25, 33, 35
bireme, 7, 9, 11, 38
birrus britannicus, 45, 79
Bitterne, Hampshire, 36, 38, 39; see also Clausentum
Blackfriars, London, ship found at, 5, 20, 31
Blussus (boatman), tombstone of, 3, 13, 35, 81
boathooks, 28 (fig 34), 29
boats, Gallo-Roman in Switzerland, 31-5; at Pommeroeul, 22-30;
    structural parts, see bilge strakes, chines, *Kaffe*, mast-step, mortise-
    and-tenon joints, nails, oars, ribs, tiller; see also clinker, carvel
Bodiam, Sussex, 38, 39
Bonn, Germany, 70
Bordeaux wine trade, 42, 51, 68
Bosiconius, *actor navis*, 43 (Tab I), 46
bottles, 70, 75-7 (and figs 60-61)
bowls, glass, 71-3; depicting Mediterranean cargo ships, 5
Bowness, Cumbria, 36, 37, 42
Bradwell, Essex, 36, 38
Brancaster, Norfolk, 36, 37, 38
Bristol, medieval trade, 63, 64, 65, 67
Bristol Channel, 39
Brough-on-Humber, Humberside, 36, 37, 38, 39
Bryggen, Norway, 62
Bugpforte, see under cargo vessels
building materials, 39; see also slate, stone
Burgh Castle, Norfolk, 36, 38
byrrus, see birrus

cabin, 27
Cabrière d'Aygues, Provence, 50
Cacerés, Spain, 49
Caer Gybi, Anglesey, 36
Caerhûn, Gwynedd, 36, 37
Caerleon, Gwent, 42, 70, 73; inscription, 41; Roman harbour, 36, 37,
    38, 40
Caernarvon, Gwynedd, 36, 37, 38
Caerwent, Gwent, 36, 38, 39, 42
Caister-by-Yarmouth, Norfolk, 36, 38, 39
Caistor-by-Norwich, Norfolk, 70
Camulodunum, 71, 72, 73; see also Colchester
Cananefates, 41
canoes (dugout), see dugout canoes
Canterbury, Kent, 63
capes, woollen, 80; see also birrus
Cardiff, 36, 37
Car Dyke, 38
cargo, 13, 62, 67-8; see also goods transfer, trade
cargo vessels, barges with inward-pointing bow and stern, 5; crew, 11;
    dugouts, 3; with open bows (*Bugpforte*), 1, 2 (fig 1); *Oberländer*
    (heavy barges), 3, 4 (fig 5); seagoing, 5, 7 (fig 11)
Carinius Gratus, T, 43 (Tab I), 45
Carmarthen, Dyfed, 36, 37, 38
carvel build, 1, 15, 25, 31
cattle, 62
caulking, 1, 16, 27, 32, 33 (fig 38)
Celtic/Continental shipbuilding, 15, 20, 23, 31, 32
Celtic deities, 42
Celtic grave with gold votive boat, 1
Chester, Cheshire, 36, 37, 38, 40, 42
Chichester/Fishbourne, Sussex, 36, 38, 39
chines, 15, 17
Classis Britannica, 37-8
Clausentum, 49, 64; see also Bitterne
Clermont-Ferrand, France, 74
clinker build, 10
cloaks, 80; see also birrus
cloth, clothing, 7 (fig 10), 13, 45, 60, 62, 67, 80
cogs, 11, 65
cohortes, Germanic in Britain, 41-2
coins, 59, 62, 65, 66
Colchester, Essex, 49, 70; colour-coated ware industry, 53, 56; samian
    workshop, 57, 58; see also Camulodunum
Colchester/Fingringhoe, 36, 38, 39
Colijnsplaat, Netherlands, inscriptions, 13, 14, 80; shippers at, 43-6,
    58
collegia, 45
Cologne (Köln), Germany, flat-bottomed amphorae from, 50; *moritex*
    from, 44; salt traders, 45; see also Köln
Cologne-Braunsfeld, glass depicting boat, 5
Colonia Claudia Ara Agrippinensis, 70 (see also Köln)
Colonia Claudia Victricensis, 70 (see also Colchester)
Commodus Ufeni(?)tis fil, 43 (Tab I), 45
Continental shipbuilding, see Celtic/Continental shipbuilding
Corbridge, Northumberland, 75
corn trade and supply, 13, 45, 62, 67
Cornelius Superstis, Q, 43 (Tab I)
costs, of transport to Britain, 49
County Hall site, London, 3rd century wreck, 5, 67
cranes, 13
cretarii, 44
crews, 7, 11-13
cunei, 41
cuparius et saccarius, 13
cups, glass, 71 (fig 53), 72 (fig 54), 73-5
Custom House site, London, waterfront, 38
customs dues (medieval), 67, 68